WHAT IS THE STATE FOR?

Coeditor-in-Chief & Publisher Deborah Chasman

Coeditor-in-Chief Joshua Cohen

Executive Editor Matt Lord

Assistant Editor Cameron Avery

Associate Publisher & Fellowship Coordinator Jasmine Parmley

Marketing and Development Coordinator Irina Costache

Arts in Society Editor Hannah Liberman

Contributing Editors Adom Getachew, Lily Hu, Walter Johnson, Robin D. G. Kelley, Paul Pierson, Becca Rothfeld, & Simon Torracinta

Contributing Arts Editors Ed Pavlić & Ivelisse Rodriguez

Production Assistants Ione Barrows & Jack Ott

Editorial Assistant Naomi Bethune

Finance Manager Anthony DeMusis III

Board of Advisors Derek Schrier (Chair), Margo Beth Fleming, Archon Fung, Deborah Fung, Larry Kramer, Richard M. Locke, Jeff Mayersohn, Scott Nielsen, Robert Pollin, Hiram Samel, Kim Malone Scott, Brandon M. Terry, & Michael Voss

Interior Graphic Design Zak Jensen & Alex Camlin

Cover Design Alex Camlin

What Is the State For? is *Boston Review* issue 2024.2 (Forum 30 / 49.2 under former designation system).

Cover art courtesy of the estate and archive of Elda Cerrato.

Image on page 7: Thomas Hawk

Mariame Kaba and Andrea Ritchie's response is adapted from *No More Police: A Case for Abolition*, published by The New Press in 2022.

Leila Farsakh's essay is adapted from *Rethinking Statehood in Palestine: Self-Determination and Decolonization Beyond Partition*, published by the University of California Press in 2021.

Leah Hunt-Hendrix and Astra Taylor's essay is adapted from *Solidarity: The Past, Present, and Future of a World-Changing Idea*, published by Pantheon in 2024.

Printed and bound in the United States by Sheridan.

Distributed by Haymarket Books (www.haymarketbooks.org) to the trade in the U.S. through Consortium Book Sales and Distribution (www.cbsd.com) and internationally through Ingram Publisher Services International (www.ingramcontent.com).

To become a member, visit bostonreview.net/memberships.

For questions about donations and major gifts, contact Irina Costache, irina@bostonreview.net.

For questions about memberships, email members@bostonreview.net.

Boston Review
PO Box 390568
Cambridge, MA 02139

ISSN: 0734-2306 / ISBN: 978-1-946511-87-4

CONTENTS

EDITORS' NOTE

WAR IS RAGING in Gaza, Ukraine, and Sudan. Democracy is under attack. And this year will likely be the warmest on record, with devastating human consequences. Everywhere we face the failures of the modern state system to prevent catastrophe.

Leading our forum, Olúfẹ́mi O. Táíwò identifies "fossil capital"—the power and resources of the fossil fuel industry—as the principal obstacle to a more just world. The problem is not only that we are dependent on fossil fuels, but that carbon has captured the state. Despite that capture, Táíwò argues, we need a "two-step" political strategy that starts with the state. And this argument sets the stage for the wide-ranging reflections in this issue: What is the role of the state in a more just future? Should social movements work inside or outside the state? What would a just state look like, and how can we get there?

Forum respondents explore the merits of Táíwò's state-centric proposal. Ishac Diwan and Bright Simons offer a realistic model for prodding states to cooperate. Mariame Kaba and Andrea Ritchie warn that power always reproduces hierarchies. Gianpaolo Baiocchi draws lessons from Latin America's Pink Tide. As many responses stress, winning elections is not enough. Change will require action and organizing at multiple scales.

Elsewhere in the issue, Leila Farsakh examines the history and fate of the movement for Palestinian statehood. Reporting from the Sudans, Joshua Craze upends the conventional view of militias as threats to state rule. Essays by Astra Taylor and Leah Hunt-Hendrix ("For a Solidarity State") and Janice Fine and Hana Shepherd ("Three Cheers for the Administrative State") offer a vision for a just state and a model for putting it into practice. And Bonnie Tenneriello documents a failure of state reform, following hard-won legislation to end solitary confinement that has done no such thing.

Plus, Richard Pithouse talks with S'bu Zikode, leader of South Africa's shack dwellers' movement, about why he'll never run for political office. Jonathan S. Blake reviews recent books by Philip Pettit, Charles S. Maier, and Natasha Wheatley. And Peter E. Gordon traces the rise and fall of theory's engagement with "real questions of suffering and social transformation."

Answering those questions is our task today. As Biaocchi concludes, "We will need to rethink what it means to engage institutions—abolishing, reforming, and reinventing them in ways that express our creativity, empower communities to decide on matters that affect them, balance inside and outside strategies, and activate popular politics."

GIANT STEPS

Olúfẹ́mi O. Táíwò

SCANNING THE twenty-first-century political landscape in 2018, essayist Rana Dasgupta issued a provocation: "The most momentous development of our era, precisely, is the waning of the nation state."

Dasgupta had in mind the global intensification of authoritarian politics, and the last six years have only exacerbated that trend. The same international system that failed to avert genocide in Bosnia and Rwanda is again allowing it in Gaza, Sudan, and with escalating risk in Ethiopia. Jair Bolsonaro has been voted out, but Vladimir Putin, Viktor Orbán, and Narendra Modi remain in office, and Donald Trump may yet win again. Meanwhile, Western and Central Africa have seen so much political upheaval that analysts have begun referring to a stretch of territory spanning the middle section of the African continent as the "coup belt." And the entire planet has already hurtled past the 1.5°C of warming that this same international system agreed to prevent eight years ago in Paris.

The response from the global left to this set of developments has been equivocal. One cluster of tendencies views the state with a skepticism ranging from pragmatic fatalism to ideologically inflected antipathy. These orientations are born of political traditions that view the state and the state system as at best an outsider's system, if not a primary antagonist. These tendencies have found expression in the street movements of the past decade and a half, from Occupy Wall Street and the Black Lives Matter uprisings in the United States to the Brazilian Free Fare Movement and the Yellow Vest protests in France.

Another set of views takes the battle over state politics to be of central strategic importance, whether as an offensive measure to wield its apparatus for progressive policies or as a defensive tactic in a war of position with colluding capitalists and the insurgent right wing. This set of views is reflected in the usual organizational subjects of the left—above all, workers' unions and labor parties, but also institutions such as workers' associations and tenants' unions—and it has found expression in the agendas of a range of popular political figures, from Bernie Sanders in the United States and Jeremy Corbyn in the United Kingdom to Lula da Silva in Brazil.

World-systems theorist Immanuel Wallerstein has described a "two-step" strategy favored by the radicals of the twentieth century: "first gain power within the state structure; then transform the world." This perspective, too, finds a present-day analogue in the ubiquity of calls for climate justice that are addressed to "policymakers"—which is to say, state managers and those in their social orbit. What's missing from this picture is the fact that states themselves, beyond corrupt individual politicians, have institutional interests in maintaining both private and state-owned fossil fuel capacity and consumption. As Fred Block argued decades ago, any serious analysis of the state must account for the structural constraints that prevent state politicians from acting against the interests of the capitalist class. Today, perhaps the most significant such constraint is the immense political power that fossil fuel interests have amassed over the last few generations. This power helps to explain the popularity of "all of the above" policies among political elites despite the clear imperatives from researchers that limiting climate change means phasing out oil and gas—not just phasing in wind and solar.

Whether to march in the streets with Extinction Rebellion, phone-bank for candidates with the Sunrise Movement, or blow up pipelines, as Andreas Malm proposes, is a tactical question. But the strategic imperative must be clear: nothing less than the total defeat of the organized political interests of oil, gas, and coal producers is necessary to make any other climate justice goals even a remote possibility. In what follows, I'll defend a twenty-first-century version of "two-step" politics: first dethrone fossil capital; then transform the world.

GETTING CLEAR about this program requires getting clear about the different positions on the nature of the state that have driven political conflict within liberation movements for centuries.

In the early nineteenth century, many high-ranking officers in the newly independent Haiti's armed forces favored joining the emerging Atlantic system and reinstituting a plantation-based economy. Dissenters among the peasant masses favored another strategy: opting instead to withdraw from the emerging Haitian state and engage in direct trade with the broader Caribbean economy.

Later that century, the split of the First International—a pioneering transnational organization that brought together communists, anarchists, trade unionists, and other leftists to advance class politics in their respective countries—owed much to a disagreement on how to relate to state power. The faction of Karl Marx and Friedrich Engels believed in contending for state power, seeing it as the engine of economic emancipation for the workers of the world. Opposite them, Mikhail Bakunin and allies held that any economic emancipation for the proletariat would come through the state's destruction, not its seizure.

A similar clash figures in what Wallerstein calls the "antisystemic movements" that upended centuries of colonial domination in the twentieth century. On one side were political nationalists who aimed to replace colonial administration with self-determined states. On the other were cultural nationalists who viewed the apparatus of the state as an impediment to cultural change.

All these schisms reflect different attitudes toward the promise and problem of state power. But behind the conflict itself lay a consensus that the state could not be ignored—and that consensus, in turn, reflects the pivotal role the state played in these centuries. In particular, the capitalist world system emerged out of trade networks built by the exploration of imperial states in the fifteenth and sixteenth centuries. The military might that secured these trade networks emerged out of both state-sponsored piracy and navies under empires' direct employ.

Whatever states are today, they are not what they once were—in part because, as Dasgupta chronicles, the state now faces serious competition for center stage in the organization of human society. Asset managers have accumulated a heretofore unprecedented share of human wealth; as of 2021, the two largest asset managers controlled enough wealth in assets to own the entire London Stock Exchange four times over. As Benjamin Braun and Adrienne Buller have put it, this means that "a handful of enormously powerful actors not only have decisive influence over the actions of the corporations in which they hold shares" but also enjoy "enormous power over the economy writ large"—an amount of power and influence that meaningfully competes with states' ability to manage and shape economic life. Where capital and the state have managed a sort of merger, it is seldom under conditions congenial to the aspirations of the antisystemic movements of the twentieth century. More often it represents the capture of public institutions by private incentives. The Chinese Communist Party, however communist it is, is an exception to which the sovereign wealth funds of Norway, Angola, and Saudi Arabia are the rule.

The role of the state in debates within liberation movements was keyed to the functional role of state power in the centuries in which these movements made their stand. State power was decisive for various conditions of possibility for broader transformations: the balance of power between competing forces within it decides the level of repression and technological development that in turn determines the possibility and efficacy of radical organizing. The throughline between nineteenth-century "stagism"—the umbrella of thought that liberation would have to come in parts with a particular order—and its later "two-step" analogue is simply one way of taking conditions of possibility seriously. Some aspects of how we organize ourselves ought to be keyed to final principles or ideals, the world we hope to build. But we may find that the world as it already has been organized prevents meaningful progress toward that ideal—or, worse, that it is organized in a way likely to wrench back every inch of progress we make.

As soon as we are prepared to concede this dismal possibility, we are but a short distance from endorsing some sort of two-step strategy; we need only ask whether the steps we would take to make the world resemble our ideal are the exact same steps that would prevent the powers that be from halting our progress. If so, our politics can happily proceed in one step: "all" we need to do, so to speak, is win elections in the political system we already have. But if not—as historically has been the rule—we will need two. Indeed, Wallerstein concludes that the reason for the eventual victory of the "two-step" strategy in twentieth-century antisystemic politics was the inability of state-detractors to produce a viable alternative to a politics that took the centrality of the state seriously.

WHAT STANDS between us and progress toward the world we want today? Increasingly, the climate itself. The very changes that are fueling extreme climactic events—record-breaking wildfires, Biblical floods and droughts—are also changing what counts as "normal" between these acute calamities. These less headline-inducing changes to average temperature directly affect the working conditions of farmworkers and logistics workers, fuel today's climate-based displacement, and drive the sea level rise and hurricane risks that threaten some of the world's largest population centers and thus help to ensure tomorrow's mass displacements. Meanwhile, the ecological disasters that drain state budgets in countries like Guyana divert resources from potential alternative economic pathways and may well grease the wheels for the promises of easy and steady revenues made by fossil capital and other extractive industries.

This is all unfortunately compatible with the hope that the tide is turning on public opinion and elite consensus about the nature of the crisis. As the Zetkin Collective has noted in conversation with Perry Anderson, every year of climate inaction strengthens the *argument* about the need for ecological justice, all while eroding the "social capacities" to convert that understanding to sensible climate policy—much less to roll back the literal tides on the basis of new ecological seriousness. The gargantuan profits that fossil fuel companies have continued to consolidate have been put to work insulating their preferred legislation and legislators from serious democratic challenge—even to the point of fueling authoritarian politics worldwide.

It should go without saying that both the causes and effects of climate change are political and economic in nature. ExxonMobil and the U.S. military alike pursued institutional strategies that supercharged emissions not out of villain-like misanthropy but out of the banal motivations of profit-seeking and self-interested state competition that link our political era to every other. The motivations that drive fossil capital as a fraction of global capital are not essentially different from those that drive any other fraction of capital, nor do state officials in the world's petrostates have entirely different motivations from those with more diversified economies.

But the extent to which climate change threatens the conditions of possibility for political organizing is not reducible to the schemes and machinations of corporations or state officials. Greenhouse gas emissions are a stock, not a flow: their ecological ramifications over the next few years will be tied much more strongly to recent decades of inaction than to any incremental policy victories the environmentally minded are able to eke out in the near future. The carbon and methane we have emitted in the past already drives the temperature changes that are displacing populations and worsening work conditions for farmworkers.

It is worth taking stock of the kind of difference this ecological reality ought to make to the prospects and priorities of people organizing in the twenty-first century. Though the idea of a "climate crisis" would have seemed foreign then, the nineteenth century was no stranger to political ecological thinking. Stagism emerged in some corners of the European left precisely around the idea of how to create the broad conditions for economic and political liberation in and across its countries.

According to "two revolutions" theorists among Russian Marxists, a first, "bourgeois" revolution was necessary pave the way to liberation.

They expected this stage to usher in political changes that matched the interests and ideological fashions of the day's bourgeoisie—including rights to free speech and assembly—alongside physical infrastructural changes that would make it easier for them to further develop the lines of commerce that had developed their political power in the first place. Furthermore, they argued that both of these developments, though emerging from the bourgeoisie's own narrow interests, would lay the foundation for a second, "socialist" revolution: one in which rights and infrastructure would be repurposed by the people. If such a transformation succeeded, then the bourgeois revolution would turn out to have been a mere stage in the longer arc of transformation from a "backward" economy to a technologically and politically advanced socialist one.

This was by no means a form of debate isolated to the Russian Marxists. Writing in the decades following the twentieth-century wave of national independence movements in Asia and Africa, economist Samir Amin proposed "delinking" as a response to the chronic economic underdevelopment of the Third World, which he characterized as "the crisis of the world-system." The newly independent states of the Third World, Amin argued, should delink from the capitalist world system by regulating external trade and capital inflows according to national level spending priorities rather than the dictates of global capital accumulation. These would include state-planned investments in national productive technologies and designed to promote egalitarian distributions of incomes between peasants and workers.

We do not need to relitigate centuries old debates between factions of the Russian Social Democratic Labour Party any more than we need to take sides in decades old debates between cultural and political nationalists of the Third World. What is worth understanding about these debates is not which side was correct, but the nature of the disputes in the first place. Under what overall historical conditions are our ultimate goals achievable in the long term, and what must we do in the short and medium term to achieve them?

TODAY, there is no Russian Tsar or Portuguese Empire to direct our strategic focus toward toppling. Instead, it is the climate crisis that threatens to hand the reins of our historical conditions to the most implacable enemies of progress and put justice out of reach. Our living and working conditions are also our political conditions, and the rise of xenophobic right-wing movements represent one valve of the political economy that the pressures of rising temperature, sea level rise, and state competition over the energy economy may flow.

A twenty-first-century "two-step" politics—fit for purpose in this environment—would involve a close cousin of Amin's view. But the delinking we must concern ourselves with is at the planetary scale: we need to delink the world economy from fossil fuels. In other words, we must achieve the energy transition.

This position is opposed from the outset to carbon reductionism—the technocratic fantasy that preventing the political crises to come consists simply in "going electric." The global rise of price-competitive renewable energy, particularly solar power, is genuinely good news. But this will not, in and of itself, lead to the phaseout of fossil fuels. The prevailing

Táíwò

definition of "energy security" used by developed countries—"a stable and abundant supply of energy," as the European Union puts it—makes the intermittency of solar and wind power a political and technical liability, which opponents of energy transition have long seized upon. While technological breakthroughs in energy storage and transmission have made it possible to provide meaningful energy security even with intermittent energy sources, enacting this possibility would require serious, coordinated investment in public energy systems.

The prognosis for our climate futures depends not only on whether we eventually reduce emissions and other ecologically unsustainable practices, but at what rate. The shareholders of ExxonMobil and the rate of return on the assets managed by BlackRock and Vanguard depend on continued fossil fuel extraction, which they have made clear themselves. We need a "two-step" solution precisely because the forces aligned against broader transformative visions will be too well resourced and well positioned to overcome if we do not first undermine the loadbearing foundation of the status quo. We must first dethrone fossil capital so that we can control enough of our political and economic system to transform everything else.

The importance of the connections between the economic and political aspects of the capitalist system's extractive bent have long been well articulated by the "degrowthers," particularly those among them defending some version of "ecosocialism." There is much to dispute about the precise manner of delinking from fossil fuels, as indicated by a well-worn series of debates about whether the ideal planetary economic system should be circular, steady state, "postgrowth," or "green growth." But any system on which fossil fuels retain their present centrality—where fossil capital has not been politically defeated one way or other—is one that is incompatible with any broader sense of justice.

This twenty-first-century "two-step" strategy is likewise opposed to a picture of climate justice that confuses the moral parity of each of our social struggles with the temporal priority of those struggles. The fact that we want to progress toward justice along a variety of interrelated axes—race, gender, class, religion—can and must inform our ultimate goals. But we must not confuse analysis of the worthiness of struggles with the practical conditions under which they become winnable. It may be that racial justice, say, simply cannot be won in a world where fossil capital still reigns. Slavery was worth opposing for every moment of the millennia for which it stood as a major mode of production before the historical door opened to abolitionism. Likewise, World War II did not make national independence movements more justified than they had been in previous generations; what it did was make them infinitely more likely to succeed than their many failed counterparts in bygone and forgotten eras. The key question is what political conditions are compatible with the breadth of changes that we want to make. And developing an answer requires taking seriously the practical constraints of our time and figuring out how to change them.

WHERE DOES the "two-step" view of twenty-first-century politics leave us with respect to the state? Climate politics is no exception to general problems with the state system, from land grabbing to elite capture; on the contrary, it is broadly illustrative of them. The considerable tools of climate policymaking, in particular, have far more often been used to organize production in ways that cement fossil fuel extraction and our present ecological trajectory. So-called "public-private partnerships" often function to subordinate the interests of the public to those of the shareholders whose financial interests are represented at the bargaining table. Warren Buffett, for one, predicts that we are soon to see a resurgence of public power in part because the private sector is eager to offload the exorbitant costs of building climate resilient infrastructure onto public balance sheets, while avoiding the legal liability associated with climate disaster.

At least in principle, state-owned sovereign wealth funds ought to strike a balance between the potential revenues from fossil fuel extraction with the overall social costs. But even these have functioned as political bulwarks for continued environmental degradation and harmful extraction, a tendency that implicates progressive Norway just as much as it does the Kingdom of Saudi Arabia (despite efforts and promises within the former to divest from fossil fuels). Tight "collaboration" between private capital and the governments of states that depend on oil revenues risks aligning elite interests in favor of perpetually increasing emissions and away from energy transition.

These are real obstacles. Nevertheless, state politics is the likeliest path forward for successful contention with fossil capital. In general, the state's decisions about what spheres of action are legal and open to the market do not simply make investments more attractive.

Rather, they create the possibility of investment in the first place under the current state system. In this way, the decisions that states make—say, expanding, contracting, or eliminating permits to drill for oil, or mandating fossil fuel phaseouts—are a crucial aspect of the "market," directing capital and social resources and shaping the trajectory of future politics.

In other words, states' capacities are not just destructive, but creative. And building a new energy system that dethrones fossil capital *and* empowers the public would be a major creative project. The state's ability to organize and plan production on a large scale would be of clear use for spurring and organizing massive energy transitions, and it could in the best cases represent a set of public alternatives to the current private finance–dominated approach to investment that puts asset managers and institutional investors in the driver's seat of climate politics. That approach, sadly, is reflected in the signature climate policy advanced under the Biden administration; as economist Daniela Gabor has argued, rather than seek to build a "big green state," it aims to "bribe private capital into fulfilling the certain policy priorities that are considered otherwise unachievable."

A more promising way forward is being charted by energy democracy movements. A town in Arkansas installed solar panels to generate electricity for its schools, revenues for the school district, and linked this effort directly with hefty $15,000 increases to previously woefully underpaid teachers' salaries. This is not a mere small-town phenomenon: the Los Angeles Department of Water and Power recently set a 100 percent renewable energy target.

Helped along by some tireless activists, the entire state of New York recently passed a Build Public Renewables Act to phase out natural gas and build state renewable capacity with "gold-standard labor language" mandating union jobs on the projects. Public power, as a larger-scale goal and also as an ethos, could serve as a tactic to force a fraction of the ruling class into supplanting fossil capital and fulfilling its revolutionary task of decarbonizing the global energy economy and decommodifying public services—much in the way that previous generations of radicals aimed to force the European bourgeoisie into its revolutionary task of replacing tsardoms and monarchies, and the African bourgeoisie into its revolutionary task of toppling European empires.

Most of these goals are far less than planetary in scope; still they fit the "two-step" model. The curtailing of emissions anywhere—but particularly in high-emitting nations—affects the drivers of hurricanes and pollution elsewhere. In this vein, the People's Agreement of Cochabamba, declared in 2010 in Bolivia, describes rich countries staying within their ecological limits as part and parcel of the "decolonization of the atmosphere." But international politics is not without relevance, of course. A dozen states have already signed on to the Fossil Fuel Non-Proliferation Treaty, including Colombia and the Solomon Islands, bolstered by statements of support from the European Parliament and the World Health Organization. Similarly, debt cancellation initiatives might well expand the flexibility that state governments have to put state resources into the proactive defense of their populations from climate crisis rather than the proactive defense of their creditors from downside portfolio risks. Each of these involves the intricate machinery of the state system, and each goes well beyond what subnational or localist climate politics can hope to accomplish. These different scales of climate politics fit together as partners rather than alternatives.

Could a twenty-first-century "two-step" politics avoid state politics altogether? It's not impossible. Leftists around the world have rightly been inspired by the resilience and accomplishments of movements in Chiapas and Rojava to carve out niches of autonomy under the nose of the state system. For thirty years, the Zapatistas have experimented with autonomous municipalities and grassroots political structures outside of the purview of the Mexican state and in the midst of serious cartel violence. Meanwhile the General Council of the Autonomous Administration of North and East Syria has formally ratified a constitution that outlines ambitious political goals that include elimination of capital punishment and gender parity throughout all governing bodies.

But if the "two-step" point of view is correct, it is *fossil capital* that we must topple in this century, not the state system or any particular state within it. Withdrawal from the state or state politics is not obviously an answer to the question of how to delink the world economy from fossil capital, unless done in a way that involves alternative energy systems on a scale that would be atmospherically relevant. After all, the emissions of ExxonMobil and the Pentagon poison the air and raise the temperature in Mexico and Syria too. Those who are skeptical of political solutions involving contesting for or with state power directly ought to explain how that abdication fits into a political trajectory that ends in the political defeat of fossil capital on a planetary scale, not simply our successful refusal to be complicit with its reign.

THE STATE we know today is rightly reviled. Its dawn was the age of colonialism, and its continued condition of possibility is a planetary system of arms dealing. Economic systems are maintained by nakedly inegalitarian decision-making structures; sovereignty is protected by an ever-expanding system of surveillance and violence, and borders are lined with razor wire. We deserve better, and we should want more. But it's the getting more, not the wanting, that is the problem.

Even a world where the state takes the side of the broad public over the narrow interests of capitalists and investors is not one that necessarily results in the changes we want. After all, as economist Minqi Li has argued, the very political shifts that would align state incentives with public ones would generate massive capitalist backlash. Can a state that advocates "degrowth" policies survive the capital flight and investment strikes that have brought state governments to heel in the past? Li argues that, at minimum, public investment would have to rise to compensate for the withdrawal of private capital; in the long run, such a model may be totally incompatible with corporate profit, implying total public ownership of the economy.

As the examples of Norway and Saudi Arabia attest, the option of highly coordinated state investment is fraught with its own dangers: the prospect of easy returns may generate a conception of the "public interest" among state managers that locks in fossil fuel expansion.

Active state intervention into twenty-first-century energy politics, whether via new nationalizations or comprehensive planning towards decarbonization, is no guarantee of a solution to the climate crisis. But it is not even a potential trajectory unless and until the state finds its interests aligned against those of capital's private owners—and on the side of the people for whom it pretends to exist and from whom it derives its resources and presumed legitimacy.

Winning the battle to align the state's interests in such a way would not deliver on justice for everyone or everything. It would not guarantee an end to racism, or sexism, it would not in and of itself undo centuries of colonial mismanagement; it would not in itself turn back the clock on generations of sedimented casteist or ableist stigma; it would neither abolish classes nor borders. But it would be a giant step—in itself a world-historical achievement, easily the task of a generation. And eventually, enough steps in the right direction get you to where you're going.

THE COLD CALCULUS OF BURDEN SHARING

Ishac Diwan & Bright Simons

TÁÍWÒ ASKS whether nation-states can be corralled to create a green global economy—a starting point, he argues, for anything else that might improve the lives of the world's poor.

As an economist and a social innovator, we see the prospect from both practice and theory, but it is important to situate the matter historically. The state was central to postwar industrialization; it has been invoked again, following the demise of the Washington Consensus, in efforts aimed at healing society from the human costs of neoliberal globalization. More recently, the call to "bring the state back" has often amounted to viewing the state as a mere platform for creative experimentation with new global governance models. We think this gets it wrong. A successful global fight against climate change will have to be based on reinvigorated states that are, if not democratic, then at least developmental.

The absence of a workable mechanism for global governance undermines the efficient allocation of the decarbonization burden.

So far, we've seen only scattered breakthroughs rather than sustained progress. This is not a new problem: multilateral processes have historically stalled on trade, development, and conflict resolution. Today's geopolitical fracturing makes any supranational steering and sanctions regime even less credible. Institutions like the Bretton Woods system, the Kyoto Protocol, the Treaty on the Prohibition of Nuclear Weapons, the Geneva Conventions, and the World Trade Organization are not a path forward; they are based principally on reciprocity rather than true globalist norms. This pseudo-governance model would be even less workable in combating climate change, since mere state-to-state reciprocity isn't practical on this issue.

How are we to overcome this collective action problem before it's too late? The most realistic option seems to be a path suggested by economist William Nordhaus, whereby "clubs"—voluntary associations of countries—take charge, each led by a large stakeholder that can internalize global externalities and would be willing to enforce trade sanctions among club members. The megastates—the EU, United States, and China—are the natural leaders here. They account for around half of global GDP as well as half of global CO_2 emissions. (China alone emitted about 35 percent of global emissions in 2023.) One can expect gaming among them on burden sharing, but that should not prevent cooperation given the high cost of inaction. Indeed, they are all moving fast—not just on decarbonization, but also in pursuit of dominance in green technology, as if they are fairly certain that these markets are here to stay.

Diwan & Simons

This still leaves 50 percent of emissions. Close allies of the three hegemons, which include all other high-income and upper-middle-income countries, account for about another 30 percent. These countries are deeply interconnected through trade relations, capital movement, and technological exchange, and in a club arrangement they would thus be likely to be disciplined by one or more of the hegemons. Europe has already instituted a tariff system, the Carbon Border Adjustment Mechanism, that will tax imports produced with brown technologies. Even if the United States or China uses subsidies instead of tariffs to attract more of the production of new technologies to their economy, other players are likely to retaliate with trade policy rather than by terminating their effort to green the planet in self-beneficial ways.

The remaining roughly 20 percent of emissions come from poorer countries, which collectively emit around 7 gigatons each year. Global attention is currently lax about their contributions, for understandable practical and historical reasons. Yet the countries in this unrestrained club will represent more than half the world population in 2050, and they could easily emit more than 10 gigatons annually by then if they are not constrained. With the climactic system increasingly sensitive to marginal shifts, emissions from this group could tilt the balance over safe temperature thresholds.

Roping in the unrestrained club is widely seen as a function of climate finance. The price tag of aligning the interests of the un-restrained club with high global ambition by funding appropriate mitigation and bankable adaptation projects has been estimated at about $1 to $2 trillion per year between 2030 and 2050. But having failed to disburse pledged commitments of just $100 billion a year, the richer countries appear in no mood to assume the full magnitude of the climate finance burden.

Yet hopes of seeing poorer countries cooperate with climate goals are not totally misplaced. For one thing, renewable technologies are becoming more affordable; solar electricity is already cheaper than fossil-based electricity at relatively low interest rates (as it is capital intensive). Moreover, poorer countries—the true Global South—will want to export to the rich North and to China, and as climate cooperation progresses, that will be possible only if these countries green their export industries—and, more broadly, their formal sectors.

Still, even in the best-case scenario, some poorer countries will fail to go green. Economically, they will be restricted, more or less, to the informal sectors of the Global South—the south of the south, so to speak. They would be joined by some pariah states specializing in "illicit" activities: the drug trade, arms sales, and tax evasion, along with coal, oil, and gas trafficking. Rich countries might be more likely to invest in police states that will restrict (climate) migration from these places than in global green development. (The EU already outsources migrant policing to Turkey and Tunisia.) In place of "fossil imperialism," then, we may end up with a new, green colonialism—a proliferation of regimes that keep poorer countries poor and specialize in stopping the barbarians at the gates, as the North would see it. A dictatorial, poor, and repressed Global South would be the price we pay for a green planet.

To avoid this dystopian result, progressive forces need to mobilize both South and North to build responsible states invested in the national common good. This is a huge undertaking, no doubt, but we see the old "state effectiveness" trope making a comeback in some of the baby steps of programs like the EU's Global Gateway. What should this responsibility look like? Responsible southern states would be developmental, refusing to limit their ambition to becoming a border police force. (Witness Botswana's "sustainable development pathway" approach or Namibia's bold plan to reduce 91 percent of its emissions by 2030 through green industrialization.) Meanwhile, responsible northern states would finance responsible southern states that are willing to pursue inclusive and sustainable development—because it's in their interest to do so. They need stronger, progressive allies in the Global South to preserve the international coalition for a rules-based normative system that is both humane and developmental. Above all, they need such alliances to offset the threats to global order posed by revanchist powers eager to align with southern states frustrated by a status quo big on rhetoric yet light on results.

This proposal may have sounded naive in the past. But in light of the realist calculus of burden-sharing clubs, it appears to be the only pragmatic and acceptable pathway for countries optimizing national interests to achieve global emissions goals.

FOSSIL CAPITAL'S ACCOMPLICE
Tara Raghuveer

FOSSIL CAPITAL has an accomplice: real estate capital. "Real estate capital" refers to investments in residential and commercial properties and related trusts. Today the level of real estate capital flowing through investment trusts and across oceans has reached a historic scale. The landlord-tenant contradiction, the inherent conflict of interests between tenants and the individuals or institutions that own their homes, is high-pitched and painful. The rent is too damn high. Most tenants don't know their landlords, who are shielded by registered agents and property managers, setting rents by algorithm from thousands of miles away to maximize profits. The state is in business with our slumlords, financing their investments through favorable loan terms, responsive to the whims of a hefty industry lobby that does not discriminate along party lines. And the state deploys eviction, a violent tool of its own invention, to protect capital's interests over public needs.

Much of this resembles Táíwò's characterization of fossil capital—brutal, all-encompassing—and it is no coincidence. Today, fossil capital and real estate capital enjoy an interconnected capture of the world economy and the state. The consolidation of the rental and utility markets create monopolistic patterns that trap people in price-gouging schemes and prevent decarbonization. At the political level, utility companies whose business models rely on fossil capital work in alliance with real estate lobbyists to block tenant protections and decarbonization regulations.

This joint capture comes with catastrophic costs. The climate crisis is the biggest displacement threat worldwide, and those displaced by climate events struggle to find housing in the communities where they land. Real estate development—involving construction machinery, transportation of materials, air conditioning, and heating systems—relies on fossil fuels, serving as an accelerant to the climate crisis. The roughly 140 million housing units in the United States cause over 15 percent of the country's greenhouse gas emissions, more than all commercial buildings combined. Over a third of U.S. households can't afford their monthly utility bills, a burden felt disproportionately by nonwhite tenants. Utility shutoffs are a leading cause of homelessness. As Daniel Aldana Cohen wrote in 2019, "In the real world, you can't separate the carbon causing the climate emergency from our physical and economic systems, any more than you can separate windows, furnaces, and air conditioners from your monthly rent bill."

When we imagine what it would take to contend against all this, it is difficult to avoid despair. But that which evokes this despair may also offer a way out. If it is true that fossil capital and real estate capital exist in a mutually supporting relationship, it should also be true that our strategies to combat them are connected, and maybe even more deeply than we have considered before.

As we conceive of the small and giant steps toward dethroning fossil (and real estate) capital, we should consider the tenant. The tenant, often also a worker, is a rarely acknowledged character in the struggle against global racial capitalism. Fossil capital—while materially impacting our lives in major ways, all the time—can feel abstracted from day-to-day life. What feels present? The abuses of real estate capital: the broken heater, the gas bill, the mold on the wall, the leaky windows, the rent. Tenants, especially poor and working-class tenants, exist at the intersection of two interlinked crises: they are the most vulnerable to climate emergencies, and they live the daily emergency of powerlessness relative to their landlords.

The union offers a fighting chance. "We deserve better, and we should want more. But it's the getting more, not the wanting, that is the problem," writes Táíwò. The getting more, the transforming the world—these ends require organizing. Not slogans, not coalitions, not email lists. Organizing. People must be politicized around their own experience, join organizations, finesse skills, make collective decisions, take action with their neighbors, evaluate those actions, and act again. This is the work of a union, whether in the context of the workplace or in the context of our homes. Tactic is what we do, strategy is why we do it; the union sharpens both. The union becomes a venue for rigorous questioning, experimentation, and refinement.

Tenant unions are among the most promising of such venues. Classically, tenant unions operate within a building, where neighbors come together to improve conditions or negotiate with landlords.

But the struggle against contemporary real estate capital, in all its twisted glory, can't be solely fought building by building. Some tenant unions—like those in Kansas City and Louisville—organize across neighborhoods and citywide; others, as in Connecticut and North Carolina, are organizing statewide.

The truth is, there is not yet a consistent practice of tenant organizing that meets the needs of our moment. But unions, like those named here, are working to change that, uniting across geography and aligning methodology to manifest their fullest potential. We tenant unionists, committed to the home as a necessary site of struggle, think of ourselves as in a similar place now to where organized labor was in the early part of the twentieth century, before mass organization and formal bargaining processes, before big money and millions of members: in a sweet but urgent spot to define what the union can be, learning from past formations and responding to our current conditions.

The scale of our twinned crises rightly fixates most of us on the state as the necessary large-scale agent for intervention. From this perspective, tenant unions and most nonstate players might be considered too small, too local, to force the state's hand or to impact fossil capital directly. But this view is anti-visionary. The grasp of fossil capital requires adversaries that will not just pose the question of how to untangle the state from capital interests, but force it to happen. Who can wield enough power to do so? Tenant unions are among the options with the most unexplored possibility. Both in their traditional form (within single buildings) and in new arrangements, tenant unions are picking bigger fights, applying more sophisticated target analysis, and creating alternatives to the existing housing market. In these moves, they can plot the course for the "delinking" Táíwò urges.

The question of the precise path forward—within the state, in relationship to the state, outside of the state, in stages—is one that can only be answered on the ground, in a union. Whatever the strategy, strategies require people to explore them; practice begets theory, not the other way around. The small step, toward the giant steps, toward transforming the world, involves trying what we haven't tried before. What if tenants can organize at scale, wielding a new kind of power in relation to their homes? What if they can do so alongside farmworkers, ratepayers, trade unionists? Could that be a winning team to take on fossil capital, real estate capital, and all that hurts us? We have to try.

LEARNING FROM THE PINK TIDE

Gianpaolo Baiocchi

I COUNT MYSELF a fellow traveler with the political project Táíwò lays out. Though he does not use this phrase, this is real utopian thinking: identifying the contours of a politics of the here and now that can be fundamentally transformative. Looking forward and back at the same time, it seeks ways to reclaim the public without going back to the technocracy, racism, and authoritarianism of the welfare state.

Where we differ lies more in the details. To solve the apparent tension between left strategies that are for or against state engagement, Táíwò updates some classic sociology with a generous "all of the above." I offer what I hope is an equally generous "yes, and . . ." rooted in the experiences of Latin America, where people have been busy experimenting with versions of a reinvented left project for the last few decades.

Beginning in the 1970s, the Latin American left reinvented itself, turning away from armed struggle and bureaucratic state socialism toward something much more plural and fluid. Movements and parties have variously emphasized national parliamentary struggle, local governance, or autonomous arenas. But one of the enduring lessons—if not the lesson—is that occupying the state is not enough. Whether we are speaking of Venezuelan Bolivarianism, Uruguay's Frente Amplio, the Zapatistas of Chiapas, or even the relatively reformist Workers' Party of Brazil, all recognized the limits of approaches premised on taking over the state.

"We know it is not enough to get to the government to then change society," reads the 1999 Brazilian Workers' Party's Program for a Democratic Revolution. "It is also necessary to change society as we get there." The idea recurs in the work of Subcomandante Marcos, former leader and spokesperson of the Zapatistas, who have inspired a generation with their ambitious experiment in liberation and self-rule in Mexico's southern region. As a famous phrase attributed to his Mountain Writings goes, "Zapatistas do not want to enter the halls of power, evict those who are there and take their place, but to break the walls of the maze of history, to leave it, and, with everyone, to make another world without exclusive rooms, doors, or keys."

Much of the debate became sharpest in the 1980s and early 1990s, when activists were facing the return to formal democracy in many countries but lacked viable left models to borrow from, given the disappointments in Eastern Europe. The context shares some similarities with the United States today: sharply increasing inequalities, a lack of credible institutional outlets for political expression, uncertainty about rights and freedoms, a precarious and splintered job market, the hollowing of public provision—alongside radical resistance and real hope in local arenas. It is not surprising that questions facing movements today—whether and how to engage political parties and institutions, whether to be part of a system that was not made for us, whether voting for the least bad option in national elections is an exercise in democracy—find so many echoes in the history of Latin American movements and parties of the era.

There are striking similarities, too, regarding the more pointed concern of whether to participate in a system founded and premised on racial subjugation. This was an explicit matter of debate among Indigenous activists when Bolivia's Movimiento al Socialismo was being formed in the late 1990s, just as it was for the Zapatistas and in Brazil's Movimento Negro Unificado in the 1980s. In the United States, these debates about the meaning of popular sovereignty found deep resonance in the idea of abolition democracy, as originally articulated by W. E. B. Du Bois: abolishing institutions of subjugation while developing others as part of a transformative political project from below.

What emerged from the debates and struggles was a set of ideas and practices of a popular left project. From Uruguay to Mexico, under various influences like liberation theology, popular education, and Indigenous thought, this was a left that centered social movements, local struggles, and radical democracy. Throughout the continent, movements attached themselves to or morphed into new parties that won municipal, regional, and legislative victories before winning national governments. Locally, regionally, and sectorally, they managed to craft fluid intersectional and socialist coalitions that embraced social justice, human rights, feminism, LGBT issues, and environmental issues in ways that would have seemed absolutely unthinkable just a few years earlier. In place of abstract theoretical debates, the focus was on practical questions about how to create "another world" in the here and now, as the slogan went. At times these movements were able to catch a glimpse of that world: a rural cooperative on collectively owned land, a local government supporting the struggles of trans sex workers, a school that introduced Indigenous language and history for the first time. In doing so, these movements pushed political horizons to new frontiers; their victories cannot be undone or erased from popular memory.

The left-of-center national governments that ultimately grew out of these earlier on-the-ground movements have achieved lots of concrete wins, even if they have not always lived up to their promises—and indeed they have disappointed on issues from extractivism to land reform, not to mention the hardening of hierarchies surrounding ruling parties themselves. We can name very real gains, whether we are speaking of the governments of Evo Morales in Bolivia, Lula in Brazil, and even the recently established tenures of Gustavo Petro in Colombia and Gabriel Boric in Chile. Thanks to this Pink Tide, as it has become internationally known, tens of millions of people have been brought out of poverty and gained access to public services. And perhaps most of all, Latin American countries have begun to face their settler and slave pasts, taking steps such as recognizing plurinationality and implementing affirmative action. This legacy is undeniable.

We in the United States today clearly do not lack the foundations of a new, radically democratic, leftist, transformative political project that draws on popular creativity and imagination—from the groundswell of activism around social housing and tenants' rights, to the resurgence of labor activism, to the courageous student antiwar activism. And as in Latin America, sterile ideological debate is often so much less important than strategic discussion, anchored in the arts of solidarity and put in the service of concrete struggles. The urgent task before us is articulating multiracial, multicommunity, and multiclass coalitions while connecting the energies of our social movements with institutional engagements in ways that do not turn those into instruments of legitimation for a broken political system.

The recent history of the Latin American popular left provides a useful template here: the center and moral compass of that popular bloc needs to be occupied by oppressed communities and their ambition to achieve social transformation. What we do not yet have is a structure of political representation—whether it takes the form or name of a party or not—that amplifies and connects these struggles, that has an institutional face, that leads by following, and that helps bring about a broader vision while enabling specific struggles. It will have to balance the choices Latin Americans have long faced—recognizing and privileging individuals or groups, formalizing or not, finding ways to remain democratic—as well as others they are coming to, such as how to face the urgency of climate change. Angela Davis has written about the need for a new political party, one "organically linked to the range of radical movements" but

> anchored in the idea of racial capitalism—it would be antiracist, anti-capitalist, feminist, and abolitionist. But most important of all, it would have

to acknowledge the priority of movements on the ground, movements that acknowledge the intersectionality of current issues—movements that are sufficiently open to allowing for the future emergence of issues, ideas, and movements that we cannot even begin to imagine today.

As we grapple with these questions, we will need to rethink what it means to engage institutions—abolishing, reforming, and reinventing them in ways that express our creativity, empower communities to decide on matters that affect them, balance inside and outside strategies, and activate popular politics. The Latin American left provides us with remarkable examples of what that kind of thinking can accomplish. Transforming the world requires nothing less.

DIVESTING FROM CARCERAL THINKING
Mariame Kaba & Andrea Ritchie

DURING A virtual convening hosted last year by Interrupting Crim-inalization, the organization we cofounded in 2018, abolitionist scholar and geographer Ruth Wilson Gilmore offered a provocation central to the question of how abolitionist organizers relate to the state: How do we, as a society, accomplish "big things" with and for people we don't know or necessarily like?

Certainly, salvaging the fate of a planet careening toward climate collapse driven by fossil fuel interests is primary among those big things we must urgently work across difference on a global scale to accomplish. Our success in doing so, as Táíwò argues, is a precondi-tion not only for our collective survival but also for achieving many liberatory goals, including futures free from violence, surveillance, policing, prisons, and punishment. As we are witnessing in horrific real time, access to rapidly diminishing natural resources and liv-able space is increasingly intensely and violently policed, from the shores of Gaza to the gold and mineral fields of the Congo to the borders of the Global North, while resistance to the forces driving extraction, climate collapse, and their consequences is increasingly violently repressed.

Táíwò suggests that these practical realities require us to, in short, stick with states: adopting a two-step strategy to first secure divestment from the fossil capital that currently structures nation-states and then to transform states into entities that structure societies committed to the survival of all. There is no question that in order to secure a just and peaceful future on this planet, divestment from fossil capital—and racial capitalism as a whole—is necessary. In 2018, for example, South African organizers described to a U.S. solidarity delegation how the failure of the emerging post-apartheid state to divest from capitalism created conditions for perpetuating policing practices reminiscent of its predecessor. This was made grimly clear in the 2012 Marikana massacre, when South African police mowed down dozens of striking Black miners, echoing apartheid-era tactics for suppression of Black labor organizing. While states remain central sites of contestation, the capital interests that control and exert power within and beyond state structures and borders are produced and perpetuated through policing. Divestment from fossil capital therefore conditions possibilities for futures beyond policing and punishment.

Yet any effort to mobilize the existing state apparatus to secure divestment from fossil capital and investment in creative capacities toward global energy transition must attend to and resist the ways carcerality inevitably barges into structures we build and rely on to collectively accomplish things big and small, from community institutions to planetary action. How do we contemplate imposing consequences for failure to adhere to collective values or goals, or to make choices consistent with our collective survival, without veering into criminalization or collective punishment? Criminalization operates in similar ways, whether it targets individual or state actors: those with the least power will experience the brunt of punishment regimes while the powerful largely escape them. Enforcement of international law and environmental regimes is no different.

In essence, creating conditions conducive to collective survival requires imagining and enacting systems of governance that will bring about not just divestment from fossil fuel interests, but also divestment from carceral logics. Otherwise the steps we take will not, in fact, bring us closer to the abolitionist futures we are fighting for.

As we argue in *No More Police: A Case for Abolition*, there is no blueprint for the abolitionist futures we're imagining and creating; we are building the world anew. There's also no consensus among prison abolitionists about what shapes these futures should take—or how we will get there. The path toward restructuring a society and economy from one built on scarcity, shaped by racial capitalism, and sustained by policing to one built on abundance, sustainable economies rooted in collective care, and transformative justice requires us to grapple and sit with many unknowns and tensions around the specifics of this transformation. As abolitionists, how do we get from where we are to the society we want to create while navigating the pitfalls along the way?

Central to this question is our relationship to the state. Should abolitionist organizers fight to move money and power from police and prisons to other state institutions like public housing, education, and health care—even though they also serve as disciplining arms of the carceral state —or do we need to work outside the state, in community-based institutions and programs? In other words, how can we extract resources currently devoted to surveillance, policing and punishment and put them toward meeting community needs and building safety without becoming a cog in a carceral apparatus? What kinds of decision-making processes do we want around how collective resources are generated and spent? How should we govern ourselves and relate to each other? In short, what is the role of the state in abolitionist presents and futures?

Abolitionists continue to grapple with questions around which economic systems and forms of governance will make space for and bring us closer to abolitionist futures. We don't all agree, nor do we have all the answers. That is not only OK; it can be generative, creating necessary space for robust debates, sharpening our analysis, and inviting experimentation, evaluation, study, and practice that will bring us closer to our vision. Contradictions and tensions are inherent in the work of worldbuilding, and many will remain unresolved, even as new contradictions emerge from the actions we take. The work of abolition is necessarily always unfinished and in process. It is essential, however, that we work together to find ways to navigate these tensions that build greater, more authentic, and grounded coherence rather than dissension and fragmentation that ultimately disempower us.

Kaba & Ritchie

ANSWERING these questions requires us to define what we mean by "the state." Ruth Wilson Gilmore and Craig Gilmore describe the state as "a territorially bounded set of relatively specialized institutions that develop and change over time in the gaps and fissures of social conflict, compromise, and cooperation." In other words, the state is a collection of institutions and practices shaped by the people who inhabit and enact them, as well as by the historical moment, place, and conditions in which they evolve, rather than a fixed structure disconnected from the people who make it up. No matter what shape states take, they represent "a claim to a right to rule on behalf of society at large"—meaning they create and enforce rules and maintain a monopoly on the legitimate use of violence to do so. They also generally have and enforce territorial limits and borders within which state institutions operate and these rules apply.

According to the Gilmores, the state secures "a society's ability to do different things," "through the exercise of centralized rulemaking and redistribution." Those things include extraction, taxation, military conscription, regulation, criminalization, surveillance, and making and facilitating profit. But they can also include building public infrastructure, providing for public education, and offering support in meeting basic needs. These functions are neither fixed nor mutually exclusive—criminalization can and does happen through state provision of public education, public health, and social programs.

This forces us to confront some larger questions: Can the state perform any of these functions without the violence of surveillance, police, punishment, coercion, and abandonment? If so, which ones? And if not, does rooting out policing require dismantling states in their entirety and putting in place different systems of governance and resource distribution?

Police and policing, and the social and economic order they manufacture and make possible, are so deeply imbricated in our conceptions and experiences of the state that it is difficult for those of us living and struggling in settler colonial carceral capitalist states to imagine them otherwise. Under what abolitionist scholar Jackie Wang describes as "carceral capitalism,"

> the state is inherently repressive. As an enforcer of contracts, it secures access to land, and represents the interests of the settler propertied class; it has a self-preserving reflex that always results in the crushing of revolution and political dissent.

Drawing on experiences studying and representing clients in state administrative systems, Dean Spade similarly characterizes the state as "a technology of extraction" that sorts, manages, and controls people, privileging some and criminalizing and abandoning others. Are these functions characteristics of carceral, racial capitalist states or inherent to all state formations? Is there an abolitionist form of "stateness" that can be mobilized to secure our collective survival and that of the planet on which it depends, or are any efforts to control the state doomed to perpetuate structures that are inherently carceral?

Kaba & Ritchie

Discerning whether surveillance, policing, punishment, and extraction are inherent to state-based governance is not simply a theoretical pursuit—it has real life implications for the goals and strategies of abolitionist campaigns. These contradictions don't have to immobilize us. Instead, we can ask ourselves what possibilities emerge if we move beyond the dichotomy of capturing or dismantling the modern Western state. What if our goal is not to seize the carceral state in an effort to transform it, but to seize power and resources *from* it to create conditions under which new economic systems and forms of governance can emerge? Recapturing the resources the state has extracted is a legitimate, and arguably necessary, means of both reducing the misery created by racial capitalism and creating conditions for abolition. And the process of securing direct, collective decision-making power over those resources is a means of practicing new forms of governance.

Practicing new forms of accountability to collective values through transformative justice rather than ceding power to the state to intervene in instances of conflict, harm, and need can lead us to better understand what individual and collective transformation is required to build abolitionist futures. Understanding the carceral state as a social relation helps us to see, in the words of nineteenth-century social anarchist Gustav Landauer, that it "is a condition, a certain relationship between human beings, a mode of human behavior; we destroy it by contracting other relationships, by behaving differently." Ruth Wilson Gilmore describes this process as rehearsal of life beyond the current carceral state.

As Grace Lee Boggs urges us in *The Next American Revolution* (2011), "we want and need to exercise power, not take it," as we transform ourselves to transform the world. There is no single way to go about this, but Boggs points to the creation of new community institutions "that give us ownership and control over the way we make our living, while helping us to ensure . . . well-being of the community and the environment," and organizing that supports the "creation of *more human* human beings and *more democratic* institutions."

For us, two things are clear: one, that the carceral, racial capitalist state cannot be reformed or captured and repurposed, and two, that abolition and racial capitalism cannot coexist. While the role of the state in abolitionist futures is in question, abolition in the now invokes a broad strategy to dismantle the carceral state and to undo settler colonialism, racial capitalism, and imperialism.

The immediate task, then, is assessing what work needs to be done to create the conditions for something new to emerge. This requires that we grapple with practical questions, such as how to organize at the community level at a scale necessary to meet collective needs in a global society in ways that do not replicate the policing functions of the state. What liberatory mechanisms of individual and mutual accountability can we imagine and practice within these projects? How might we preserve collective resources for the common good against those who would seek to accumulate them for private gain or put personal preference above collective goals? How do we navigate strategic questions focused on limiting the state's power to do harm and maximizing its capacity to meet collective needs while practicing and fighting for more participatory forms of governance?

Kaba & Ritchie

As we do so, we must be wary of the traps inherent in making demands that give the state power over their realization. In other words, we need to go beyond winning concessions from the state—we need to develop capabilities to govern ourselves, and our planet, otherwise.

NO SUBSTITUTE FOR STATE POWER
Joe Guinan & Martin O'Neill

TÁíwò IS RIGHT that what Wallerstein called the "two-step" strate-gy—"first gain power within the state structure; then transform the world"—looks harder to achieve than ever in our world of unfolding climate calamity. But is Táíwò's updated first step—dethroning the exorbitant and deadly power of fossil capital—any easier to achieve than Wallerstein's? We agree that fossil capital must be dethroned, but we are not sure how far this alternative takes us.

Decarbonization ultimately requires a sustained and deliberate act of capital destruction on a scale about twice that of the end of slavery. As with the abolition of slavery, it is an inescapable moral imperative—a precondition for a livable human future. But neither capitalists nor state managers have yet shown themselves sufficient-ly willing to change their behavior in the face of the climate crisis. And while we strongly support nonstatist solutions to create local forms of energy democracy, on their own they do not seem capable of displacing fossil capital on a feasible timeline. The staggering scale of the problem seems to call for the deployment of state power, under the direction of socialist or social democratic political forces. Yet such forces seem far away from being able to exercise or compel such radical state action, which seems to bring us back to where Wallerstein started.

In other words, Táíwò's two-step may simply be Wallerstein's in disguise. If this is right, the old problem of securing state power really cannot be sidestepped.

Things might look different if the state had less power than it used to, but the "waning of the nation state," as Dasgupta put it, was always oversold. Neoliberalism denigrated the state in theory, and it allowed capital to slip the leash of state-based tax-and-spend policies. In practice, however, it relied on the state to enforce private property rights and insulate market measures from democratic politics. It rolled back social democracy and socialism precisely because it rolled back democracy. Rather than dismantling the state, neoliberalism repurposed it, whether as market-maker (via privatization), regulator, or as ameliorative manager of social relations. And the state has remained central to the economic governance and management of capitalism, especially since the 2008 financial crisis—and even more so during the COVID-19 pandemic.

The state remains as powerful as ever—and *only* the state has the regulatory and planning capacity to intervene at scale and in the manner required to manage the climate crisis and the transition to a decarbonized economy. After all, the throne room of fossil capital is guarded assiduously. Without the concentrated deployment of collective political power that the state makes possible, we are left with the inadequate pantomime of market-based approaches. And as Táíwò no doubt agrees, all such approaches have failed to deliver climate action that is swift or deep or large-scale enough to avert impending calamity. The price mechanism, in particular, is inadequate to the task, as Brett Christophers persuasively argues in his recent book, *The Price Is Wrong: Why Capitalism Won't Save the Planet* (2024).

By contrast, the historical record tells us clearly that the state *can* wield its power to discipline capital and meet existential threats. As talk of a Green New Deal evokes, the state successfully redirected the productive capacity of the U.S. economy under FDR. During World War II, the state engaged in even more direct economic planning, using instruments such as price controls and rationing. And the U.S. state has a long and creditable—though sometimes underappreciated—history of nationalizing politically obstructive capital interests. Similar moves were achieved in Britain under Clement Attlee, with steel and coal nationalization as well as the creation of the National Health Service. The point is that democratic governments have exercised sufficient power in the face of grand challenges in the past, and they can do so again.

Of course, the track record of state action on climate has not been encouraging—at least in the West. The responses of governments of Western democracies seem always too little, too late. As Gus Speth recounts in *They Knew: The U.S. Federal Government's Fifty-Year Role in Causing the Climate Crisis* (2021), the U.S. government has known about but ignored or buried evidence on climate change for at least five decades—what Speth calls "the greatest dereliction of civic responsibility in the history of the republic."

Moreover, even in its boldest forms, existing climate action in the United States and Europe falls severely short for the reason Táíwò identifies: it requires the consent of capital, which at best permits inadequate nudges through regulation, price mechanisms, incentives, and derisking. Incentives to maximize financial returns still predominate over incentives actually to decarbonize, and in a context where capital has learned to manipulate, co-opt, capture, and outmaneuver state oversight, especially through the tax code, "greenwashing" is a pervasive risk. Green subsidies under Biden's Inflation Reduction Act are flowing to oil companies that continue to extract fossil fuels, for example—hardly a forceful nudge. There is a serious argument for delivering a knockout blow to the fossil fuel industry through nationalization, an approach that could seek to combine a program of state-directed planned decarbonization with the liquidation of the fossil fuel lobby as political actors.

The trouble is not that we lack a plausible vision of how to use state power to enact a just, green transition. The political left in the United States and Europe already possesses the main elements of an ecosocialist agenda capable of doing so. This includes bold and comprehensive economic planning, of the kind that democratic states undertake during times of total war, and alignment with the interests of working people to ensure a just transition. Indeed, the policy platforms of Jeremy Corbyn and Bernie Sanders had already laid out the beginnings of the steps that need to be taken.

Instead, the central issue we face is how state power can be secured and deployed to carry out this agenda. The Chinese Communist Party is in a rather different position, but in the hollowed-out democracies of the West—absent a popular rev-olution—there is simply no substitute for winning democratic control over the state.

So what's the path forward? The electoral defeats of Corbyn and Sanders—and the intense hostility that they encountered from the political center—show that it is not enough to articulate a viable economic strategy when the balance of political forces is so solidly arrayed against it. Large chunks of the liberal, centrist camp are simply not willing to work as junior partners in a left-led political alliance, even if the cost is electoral losses to the neopopulist right. The left must face this fact head on as it builds a strategy to win. The task constitutes a generational challenge, but it must be done.

COMPLICATED PLACES
Claudio Lomnitz

THE PROJECT that Táíwò envisions—dethroning fossil capital—raises hard questions about the current state of the state. It may be that in the United States, "state politics is the likeliest path forward for successful contention with fossil capital." But what about state structures that look far too weak for purposeful collective action? We might think of political sociologist Fernando Escalante's useful distinction between "bureaucratic republics" and "mafioso republics," as well as anthropologist Clifford Geertz's assessment of the patchy development of sovereignty in what he called "complicated places," but I'll focus on the transformation of the state in one national society: Mexico.

Set in motion by the corrosion of an old system of public order and neoliberal structural reforms, a new state form emerged in Mexico in the 1980s. It has consolidated since then, outlasting neoliberalism's hegemony. The core quality of the new state is an excess of sovereignty and a dearth of administrative capabilities; state development has been marked by increased centralization of power in the hands of the president of the republic and a diminished ability to keep transaction costs steady and predictable. Indeed, because the state's mechanism for regulating and protecting economic transactions has been transformed, the modus operandi of the new state is especially evident in the ways that policing is organized, and it is worth starting there.

Over the course of the twentieth century, the Mexican state developed a system of governance that was based on extracting the resources required for public safety directly from those who broke laws, or from those who wished to guarantee their application. In other words, public safety was financed through bribery and extortion, much more than through taxes. Local police forces regulated informal markets and protected property rights selectively. The state compensated for its disproportionately small tax base by combining oil revenue with direct levies for various public services, including policing. (Even today, Mexico's tax-to-GDP ratio is the lowest among OECD countries, indeed less than half the OECD average.)

Policing was thus paid for by the public directly, either by way of bribes offered in exchange for tolerance or of rents paid by local businesses in return for protection. The state also used the police force as a lever to swap toleration of informal economic activities for political support. At the same time, limits to police voracity and extortion were set politically by Mexico's one-party authoritarian state, enhancing predictability and thereby creating a feeling of order and relative safety. This was the system that prevailed roughly between the 1930s and the mid-1980s.

Then came global oil and financial crises, and the Mexican state started to break down in the wake of neoliberal reform, free trade, and a surge in drug-trafficking revenue following Mexico's entry into the cocaine business in the mid-1980s. But these systemic pressures pulled in opposite directions.

On the one hand, trade liberalization—which came into full bloom with the passage of NAFTA in 1994—required the development of the rule of law, secure property rights, and predictability of transaction costs. As a result, trade tended to promote the development of a professional police force, paid for through taxes rather than by extortion. And indeed, starting in the 1990s, the Mexican state began investing heavily in the professionalization of its police forces.

On the other hand, North American integration and free trade also fostered the development of organized crime, initially built around the drug trade—which went from being family businesses to sophisticated corporations with hundreds and even thousands of employees. Mexico's comparatively low level of police regulation led organized crime to gravitate southward, away from the United States, where its operational capabilities could be more easily secured. The consolidation of organized crime was further facilitated by Mexico's democratic transition; the end of the Institutional Revolutionary Party's one-party rule in the early 1990s led political candidates and parties to compete for illegal drug money, which had the special advantage of flowing in cash. The political clout of organized crime thus increased with democratic competition.

The dynamic tension between these two forces—the push for the rule of law, and the growing nexus between organized crime and politics—gave rise to a new kind of state.

One of the effects of this enduring dynamic is that agents of the Mexican state today frequently find themselves in a position of self-disavowal and self-misrecognition. Indeed, the state faces considerable difficulties coordinating its agencies—a characteristic on display in the chronic mistrust between the Mexican military and its various police forces, which led Mexico's president, Andrés Obrador, to dissolve the old Federal Police and fold it into a newly created National Guard operating under direct military control.

But policing is always a local business, so shootouts between state and municipal police forces occur regularly, and investigative policing, which was never efficient in Mexico, has broken down completely. Homicides and forced disappearances go almost entirely uninvestigated. Mexico today is a highly militarized state with almost no capacity to investigate or deter serious crimes.

Moreover, the state's self-estrangement—its Kafkaesque horror at having metamorphosed into an alien creature—spurs further concentration of power. Obrador regularly portrays himself as the only reliable agent in what is otherwise a flailing and uncoordinated set of dubiously public institutions. The president and the army are thus elevated above the rest of the state, as if they were guarantors of the interests of the people, but the renunciation of supporting local policing, and the mistrust of the judicial apparatus as a whole actually serves further to ensconce the power of organized crime, which has so diversified its activities that it now plays a central role in the everyday regulation of the economy.

At this stage, then, the Mexican left faces a steep uphill battle to advance any progressive program, including divesting from fossil fuels. At a minimum, doing so will require strengthening the state's administrative capabilities and wrenching control of public goods, including security, from the clutches of organized crime, which may be the biggest challenge of all.

ORGANIZING IN AND OUT OF THE STATE
Thea Riofrancos

IN ITS BROAD STROKES, I find Táíwò's exhortation—"first dethrone fossil capital; then transform the world"—compelling. Fossil capital stands in the way of all manner of progressive priorities—both because there is no just society on a scorched planet and because fossil capital is a form of political domination, increasingly allied with a neofascist right. In this context, we need the state both for its disciplinary power (what other institution could enforce a phaseout and eventual ban on fossil fuels?) and for its infrastructural capacities (it is hard to imagine an energy transition at scale without public money and even public ownership).

But how can the state serve as both executive committee of fossil capital and righteous protagonist for climate justice? And what mix of social forces and political strategies would prove most decisive in this fight? As I see it, these are really the same question. Dethroning fossil capital can only be achieved by concerted organizing. Attempting to assign "temporal priority" to a political goal—even one as imperative as a livable biosphere—runs into the classic chicken-and-egg dilemma of any radical struggle to make the world anew.

In other words, the "two steps" in Táíwò's update of Wallerstein must be as parallel as they are sequential. If one foot takes a step into state power, the other must deal a blow to its current forms. And this dance must occur on both sides of the porous divides between state and society, economy and polity. When the left ascends to government, it must not only confront the capitalist class as an external constraint but deftly evade and root out what Juan Carlos Monedero has called "snipers in the kitchen": the many forces within the state's variegated terrain, from the judiciary to the repressive apparatus, that undercut the ability and efforts of progressives in power to take on fossil capital. Given the sway of our opponents over the organs of government, triumph at the ballot box is not enough. Alongside electoral victories and legislative dealmaking, it took sophisticated coordination of forceful protest and mutual aid to get the Build Public Renewables Act passed last year in New York. These tactics are often seen as clashing, but in reality they are complementary. Policy wins are never simply the result of shrewd backroom politicking once progressive technocrats take office. They depend on organized pressure from outside the state.

These lessons also translate to any campaign to phase out fossil fuels—a goal that Táíwò correctly contends would require the strong arm of the state. I agree that there is a clear role for government mandates in restricting the supply of coal, oil, and gas. A broad range of policy options are available: ending fossil fuel subsidies; banning new extraction; and on the more ambitious end, nationalizing oil companies to ensure just transition for workers and the communities they support. But as vital as government action is, state officials cannot battle fossil capital alone.

One reason is speed. Public policy takes time, which is precisely what we do not have. The reality of a boiling planet requires immediate direct actions that disrupt the extraction and distribution of fossil fuels at critical chokepoints. Drilling rigs, offshore platforms, and vast networks of pipelines are sunk costs. A campaign of concerted sabotage that impedes the profitability of these assets could quickly drive a wedge between financiers and fossil fuel firms, as Andreas Malm has persuasively argued. And as proponents of nationalization as a route to phaseout have proposed, crashing the value of these investments would ease a government takeover.

Here too, government policies and movement tactics could work in tandem. Ending subsidies cuts into profits, as does blockading, occupying, or sabotaging physical plants; in the face of compounding action, desperation might weaken fossil fuel's resistance to state takeover—and would certainly lower the price tag of compensation, should policymakers decide to soften the blow. (Or they could go Salvador Allende's bold route: when the democratically elected socialist leader nationalized U.S.-owned copper mines in 1971, he deducted "excess" profits from their valuation, effectively canceling out any expected compensation.)

Such coordination between radical movements and their allies in the state might seem far-fetched at this moment. But the same could be said about all transformative processes before they took

Riofrancos

hold. Six months ago, I would not have predicted that an unprecedented, monthslong mobilization in solidarity with the cause of Palestinian freedom would bring well over a million Americans into the streets, including most recently nearly 400 demonstrations on college campuses. While the protests have not yet secured their immediate goal of a permanent ceasefire, they have certainly had an impact. Relentless organizing has finally pushed Biden to threaten to withhold U.S. weapon shipments, helped shift public opinion, pressured some institutions to divest, forced politicians to choose sides, and, most dramatically, called into question the president's reelection in November.

What set of conditions could occasion a similar level of mobilization and militancy to pressure the state, from without and within, to "delink" from fossil capital and embark on an energy transition at speed and scale? It is admittedly hard to say, but this is the question we need to ask. The United States has seen massive climate demonstrations. Some 4 million around the world took part in protests in September 2019. (The largest U.S. gathering was in New York City, which saw 250,000 people turn out.) But it's equally clear that the climate crisis has not seen the level of mobilization and militancy as either the George Floyd uprising or the ongoing Palestine solidarity movement. This is despite the abundance of opportunities: the United States is the top oil and gas producer on earth, and potential physical targets are myriad. Episodes of fierce resistance such as the ultimately brutally repressed protest camp at Standing Rock or the ultimately successful movement to prevent the Keystone XL pipeline are illustrative in their relative exceptionality.

One might conclude that extreme weather events—as deadly and as intertwined with both racial capitalism and imperial violence as they are—do not have the same galvanizing effect as spectacular episodes of state brutality. But side-by-side comparison has its limitations. The dramatic moments of social unrest in the summer of 2020 and again today are not isolated cases but rather two moments along the same trajectory. It's hard to imagine American youth connecting the dots between apartheid and segregation, between policing and occupation—or calling to defund the carceral state then and divest from the Israeli state now—without the three prior cycles of protest against police brutality.

Could the lessons that protesters are learning today—analysis of tactics and targets; messaging discipline and communal care; political education and intersectional coalitions—be preparing them for pitched battles with fossil capital on the other side of the horizon of current possibilities? We can't know the answer today, but the future of the planet depends on it being yes.

DOING THE UNPRECEDENTED

Olúfẹ́mi O. Táíwò

THESE RESPONSES raise challenging and clarifying points. A major fault line in the discussion concerns the political scale—and thus the set of actors—we should focus our attention on in order to make atmospherically relevant change.

The widest-angle view is the supranational level. Diwan and Simons see an important role for cooperation among states; at the same time, they argue that recent efforts to "bring the state back" have not taken the state seriously enough. Since states are not reciprocally situated when it comes to climate change, we should not expect much from multilateral diplomacy (à la Kyoto) or new models of global governance (à la the WTO). Our best chance, they think, lies with a more "responsible" version of the "club" path proposed by Nordhaus.

I also think the Nordhaus plan, in its pure form, represents a failure mode of climate politics—likely to lead to "dystopia," for reasons that Diwan and Simons trace out. Kaba and Ritchie further illuminate why: state imperatives are fundamentally defined by the stick of carcerality. It is thus no surprise that state managers in the Global North interpret their interests in a way that leads dollars away from sustainable development and in the direction of border policing. Migration enforcement arrangements like those between the EU and Tunisia or between the United States and Mexico represent the grim distributional politics of "clubs" that aim not to prevent climate impacts, but to concentrate their worst effects on the most marginalized among us—exactly the logic of carcerality as Kaba and Ritchie lay it out. The "progressive forces" that Diwan and Simons say must mobilize to avoid this result—by building more responsible states across both North and South—will have to be clear-eyed about how the state defends itself.

We have now moved one scale down to states themselves. Guinan and O'Neill also have this sort of focus, arguing that local forms of energy democracy aren't large enough to displace fossil capital on their own.

I broadly agree: state power is the most plausible route to challenging fossil capital, which would make my perspective on the central political question of the twenty-first century not altogether unlike Wallerstein's perspective on that of the twentieth. But Guinan and O'Neill focus on the political realities in the United States, the UK, and "the West." Would it make a similar difference to global ecological prospects if electoral elements of the state of Togo or of El Salvador were won to the cause of ecosocialism? One reason to suspect not is that the state, as such, is less important to the global cause of defeating fossil capital than what (some) states can do. Winning elections without getting sufficient support for the specific project of decarbonization will not get us any closer to climate justice than we are now, whether those elections take place in Britain or Botswana.

This takes us to yet another scale: the grassroots politics and political cultures blossoming across states and underneath them. Baiocchi draws our attention here, highlighting activists and movements that stayed focused on practical questions rather than getting drawn into theoretical debates. And with the case of Mexico, Lomnitz shows that some of the important practical questions are not simply about seizing state power but expanding the state's basic capacities.

There is a lesson about political culture here: the ethos of the world we seek to build by way of the state should also be cultivated in the state itself. That means we should be attempting not just to wield the levers the state has built for itself but to create institutions within the state that are responsive to popular goals. Baiocchi's example of the Brazilian Workers' Party was significant in this sense, too: its call for "participatory budgeting" in the 1980s meaningfully transformed the character of state power in Brazil. This model of democratic empowerment has since been adopted worldwide and is already being used to address climate change at local and regional scales.

I strongly agree with these reminders to attend to practical constraints, and it's in that spirit that I am trying to displace moralizing questions about what kinds of violence the state may be complicit in with practical ones. What political approaches will do the job of destroying fossil capital, and on terms that are compatible with the worlds we want? I suspect that exactly this tension between moralizing questions and practical ones loomed large in some of the examples Baiocchi points to: for instance, the question of "whether to participate in a system founded and premised on racial subjugation" debated by the Zapatistas, Bolivia's Movimiento al Socialismo, and Brazil's Movimiento Negro Unificado. We can take inspiration from the way each movement resolved that tension into action—whether in the form of participation in state politics or calculated withdrawal into another set of effective possibilities.

Next door to a focus on grassroots politics is a focus on the dynamic co-creation of grassroots and state-level politics, which Riofrancos describes. Campaigns to phase out fossil fuels will likely require the levers of the state, but it's hard to imagine them being pulled from under the noses of fossil fuel lobbyists and bought politicians without serious concerted political pressure from elsewhere. She notes that at least some of the wins we have seen so far, like the Build Public Renewables Act in New York, involved intentional coordination between outsider pressure politics and the boring bureaucracy of state legislatures. Ecuador provides an even grander example: after ten years of campaigning by Indigenous, youth-based, and other grassroots organizations, people voted in a referendum last year to stop all extraction and oil exploration in Yasuní National Park. Of course, it's a big leap from success even at the scale of a large state to making a global difference. But taking on the task of defeating something on the scale of fossil capital requires setting out to do the unprecedented.

The means for doing so might well be unprecedented themselves—or, at least, new variations on old themes. All of the respondents acknowledge this to some degree or another, but I think Raghuveer offers a particularly interesting way forward. Fossil capital shows up in the lives of most people in the way we meet our most basic needs, including housing. When it comes to organizing political power around preserving the ecology that sets all of our living conditions, it may be that the way forward is refreshingly direct: supporting people organizing around their living conditions.

Raghuveer reminds us of the difference that organizing makes. Through it, people practice doing politics, develop the skills and connections required to do it well, and get opportunities to think with others about what they want and how to get it. These are preconditions for political success on any scale, and the global scale is no exception. It may well be the sort of thing the Brazilian Workers' Party had in mind when it spoke of the need to "change society as we get there"—the kind of small steps that giant ones are made out of. ◆

Militia members in Iraq's Popular Mobilization Units (PMU). Image: Ahmad Al-Rubaye/Getty Images

RULE BY MILITIA
Joshua Craze

IN APRIL last year the Rapid Support Forces (RSF) clashed with the army in Khartoum, beginning a civil war that has plunged Sudan into humanitarian crisis. Over ten million people have been displaced, and almost half the country faces acute hunger. For the warring parties, catastrophe has proved profitable: both have seized humanitarian assets, taxed aid convoys, and looted the civilian population. Once an ethnically organized militia beholden to Omar al-Bashir, the dictator who ruled the country between 1989 and 2019, the RSF has begun to grow into a transnational economic empire; it already has a gold mining business offshored in the United Arab Emirates and forces that have deployed in Libya and Yemen. Eager to complete this transformation, the group is now intent on capturing the state that created it.

Militias are often taken as a sign of weak or absent government, the result of renegade actors operating in the wake of state collapse. Such a narrative could be told through a roll call of fallen dictators—from Mohamed Siad Barre in Somalia through to Saddam Hussein in Iraq and Muammar Gaddafi in Libya—whose removal seemed to result in the death of the state and the emergence of militias that pick over its carcass. But these lapsarian lessons about the evils that befall a society after state collapse occlude more than they reveal. The reality is that many militias active around the globe today were created by states. In the aftermath of the economic crises of the 1980s, governments wracked by debt found militias an efficient way of managing restive populations.

Sudan's story is exemplary. When Bashir came to power in a coup, he faced International Monetary Fund (IMF)–imposed austerity and an expensive civil war in the south of the country. His solution to both problems was to invent a durable form of rule by militia. Bashir privatized much of the state, selling it off on the cheap to his cronies in the security organs, while withdrawing services from the country's peripheries. He also privatized the civil war, outsourcing most of the actual fighting to ethnically organized militias. These forces secured control of Sudan's oilfields, while enriching themselves through looting and extortion. Bashir's mode of entrepreneurial predation was a grim analogue to the well-documented neoliberal privatizations that prevailed in the Global North in the 1990s and led to the violent policing of populations abandoned by the state.

Today, the RSF's attempted takeover of Sudan is just one example of a series of recent militia campaigns that have contested state power across the globe. Just like the states they have attempted to overthrow, contemporary militias operate at the interstices of global supply chains, controlling resource flows—gold in Sudan and the Central African Republic (CAR), and oil in Libya—and exploiting the populations under their control. Yet even if these militias have challenged the state, this should not blind us to the fact that they have also enabled state power.

These arrangements are at odds with the normative assumptions of liberal peacemaking, which undergird cookie-cutter, UN-backed Security Sector Reform (SSR) processes in every postwar settlement in the Global South. The central tenet of SSR is that a state should have a single unified army and a monopoly of violence within its territory. Its motto might as well be: *where the militias are, the state is not.* That assumption has been proven false, time and again. In South Sudan, for example—now five years into an SSR process that began in the aftermath of civil war—the state has ruled by multiplying militias. Far from preventing the state from functioning effectively, militias have proved essential to its continued existence.

Indeed today's militias, simultaneously state-supported armies and private economic actors, are the substantive political force organizing much of our world, even if the international system still insists that the nation-state is its operative political unit. These militias are not aberrations, nor are they atavistic forms of social organization. They flourish because of the way that nation-states are inserted into the contemporary global economy.

IN 1919 Max Weber could confidently assert that the state is the community "that claims the monopoly of the legitimate use of physical force within a given territory." Even as a normative claim—to say nothing of political reality—this was a relatively new idea. For much of European history, militias and other nonstate military actors played a part in state policy. Feudal military mobilization, for example, largely relied on assembling coalitions of aristocratic houses and their levies. When this system broke down, it was replaced by a marketplace for mercenaries in which access to force depended on capital reserves. By the eighteenth century, half the Prussian army was comprised of hired troops, and all the European states except Switzerland relied on foreign fighters. These mercenaries were sometimes drawn from private armies. Just as often, European rulers would hire out their own forces to other sovereigns.

Privatized violence allowed the state to act with relative impunity. In times of conflict, privateers were licensed to attack the state's enemies, though they could be disavowed if they caused their patrons problems. The Elizabethan Sea Dogs spent the second half of the seventeenth century razing and extorting Spanish colonial cities, netting their backers in London, including the Queen, a handsome profit. When one of the most famous Sea Dogs, Walter Raleigh, attacked one colonial settlement too many, he was executed to appease the Spanish ambassador.

Prior to the nineteenth century, private violence did not oppose state violence, but was all too often a means of its expression. Behind the bandits, to paraphrase French historian Fernand Braudel, stood the lords who bankrolled them. Privateers and mercenaries were only two types of nonstate armed actors that could be found in Europe. One could also mention mercantile firms (the British and Dutch East India companies among others), bandits, religious groupings, and almost constant rebellions against the violent extractive power of the state.

The state itself was just one of many forms of military power that vied with each other, none of them necessarily more legitimate than any other. If the state won, it was because, as Charles Tilly puts it in his famous article on state- and war-making, "small groups of power-hungry men fought off numerous rivals and great popular resistance in the pursuit of their own ends, and inadvertently promoted the formation of national states." In this telling, Weber's legitimation of state violence was the winner's prize bestowed on the most distinguished group of bandits. The state became the form that seized the mode of predation.

Other groups were to be eliminated. By the nineteenth century, states were creating mass conscription armies, privateers were banned following the Paris Declaration in 1856, and neutrality laws prevented many countries' citizens from fighting in foreign forces. Writing in the aftermath of World War II, the German legal theorist Carl Schmitt could look back with nostalgia to the establishment of the *jus publicum Europeaum*: an interstate European order that, he claimed, bracketed warfare by making it the prerogative of states and thus curbed the brutality of the religious and factional wars of the sixteenth and seventeenth centuries. Such a European order, Schmitt realized, was only thinkable in relation to what he termed the "vast free spaces" of the rest of the globe, which would become the stage for displaced European antagonisms and land and resource appropriation. European banditry had moved house.

ONE OF ITS new homes would be in Africa. During the nineteenth and the first half of the twentieth century, in many of the places where militias now flourish, the state tended to be a weak colonial occupying power, reliant on setting extant local forces against each other and intent on seizing what it could from the populations it tried to control.

In what became South Sudan, the history of the state is the story of the region's violent inclusion within the global marketplace. Since the nineteenth century, the territory has experienced a series of incursions by foreign powers. Slavers, financed by Khartoum, were followed by a Turco-Egyptian occupation and then a British colonial administration that began in 1899 and lasted until Sudan's independence in 1956. The details of these occupations differed, but certain elements remained constant. Seen from southern Sudan, the state was an emissary from elsewhere, and like the humanitarian agencies that now work in the region, it was answerable to the priorities of distant capitals, not to the southern Sudanese people. Colonial government was little interested in developing the region. Instead, successive regimes armed militia forces from among the area's many ethnic groups, setting them against each other, while using patrols to capture conscripts and force the payment of tithes (a tactic used by Sudanese slavers and British colonial officers alike). Local leaders instrumentalized the colonial regime, using its guns and resources to defeat competitors and punish resistant populations. It paid to be on the right side of the biggest bandit in the region.

Colonial violence often followed the paths created by the needs of international commerce. As Peer Schouten has shown, a surge in European demand for ivory in the nineteenth century led to the creation of long-distance trade routes in Central Africa. Caravans taking ivory and other resources required security, which necessitated the payment of protection fees. Entire communities would uproot themselves to be better positioned at crucial nodes of this transport system, and an elite emerged, perched along the ivory routes. The entrance of colonial capital did not just empower some communities at the expense of others (who were attacked, controlled, or displaced), but fundamentally changed the exercise of political power, which became orientated around a *hongo* (transit tithe) economy. Rather than being constituted by internal community dynamics, political power was to be found in harnessing and exploiting external forces. Schouten sees this as a process of "extraversion," a term coined by French political scientist Jean-François Bayart to conceptualize how African elites, rather than being dominated by the continent's subsidiary position within the global economy, came to actively participate in it, reimagining their subsidiary position for their own ends.

In parts of Central Africa, the *hongo* economy came to a close in the late nineteenth century due to the creation of large infrastructural projects—including railways—that saw the colonial powers seize control of transport routes. Nevertheless, the ambitions of the colonial state were always quite limited. In a Dutch cartoon of Leopold II from the period, the founder and sole operator of the Congo Free State is depicted as a roadblock operator, and the colonial state appears to be running a protection racket, taxing trade and exploiting civilians much like a contemporary militia.

In what was to become the CAR, the French state ruled indirectly by empowering militia leaders, who used the colonialists' weapons to enslave and tax the populations under their control. As Louisa Lombard suggests, the colonial state, like the militia leaders it empowered, was more interested in extracting value from the circulation of people and things than it was in establishing a delimited territory and maintaining a monopoly of violence.

These colonial histories are not comprehensive but indicative. They suggest that far from being an exception to an unbroken history of Weberian statecraft, militias form part of a longue durée in which states often outsourced fighting to local militias that both instrumentalized and resisted foreign incursions. Many of the places where one today finds rule by militia are marked by such histories. Perhaps, these histories further suggest, the state's monopoly of violence was only a brief period in European history—one with specific geopolitical coordinates that are now coming apart.

ONE KEY characteristic of contemporary militias is that though they are often backed by the state, their legitimacy is almost always derived locally. The origins of Sudan's RSF can be traced to the Janjaweed (a portmanteau word in Sudanese Arabic that roughly means "devil horsemen") militias of Darfur. During the 1990s, there was intermittent conflict between largely sedentary agrarian non-Arab populations and transhumant pastoralist Arab groups, many of which had fled drought in Chad during the 1980s. In 2003 these low-intensity clashes were transformed by the beginning of Darfur's rebellion, after non-Arab groups rose up to protest their marginalization at the hands of Bashir's government.

Khartoum gave the Arab pastoralists political and military support, creating the Janjaweed militias. In so doing, Bashir transposed a political struggle onto an ethnic distinction as a means of fighting a counterinsurgency on the cheap. Bashir's control of the Janjaweed was never absolute. While they waged his war, killing civilians, looting livestock, and displacing some two million Darfuris, they did so for their own ends, occupying non-Arab land and assassinating their political opponents. By 2013 discontent was growing amongst the Janjaweed, who demanded development projects—schools and hospitals—from the central government, much like their erstwhile enemies in the Darfuri rebel groups. Bashir responded by marginalizing or imprisoning key Janjaweed leaders and promoting Mohamed Hamdan Daglo, nicknamed Hemedti, a young camel trader turned militia leader, to run a formalized version of the Janjaweed, the RSF, whose initial six thousand members were largely drawn from Hemedti's own Mahariya branch of the Rizeigat Arabs and whose leadership was composed of his family members.

In South Sudan, the militias used by the government also have local sources of legitimacy. After a 2005 peace agreement brought an end to Sudan's twenty-two-year-long civil war, the Sudan People's Liberation Movement/Army (SPLM/A), which had fought against Khartoum and was poised to take over a southern regional government, faced a problem. The biggest fighting force in southern Sudan was not the SPLA (then the SPLM's military wing) but the largely Nuer—the region's second largest ethnic group—militias that Khartoum had used to control the oilfields. Salva Kiir, the head of the SPLM, feared that Bashir would use these militias to disrupt a referendum on southern independence scheduled for 2011. So in 2006, newly flush with oil revenues flowing into the southern regional government, Kiir bought off the militias, offering them positions within a national army. This integration was formal rather than substantive, with the militias remaining answerable to their own leaders. Many SPLM commanders feared these newly integrated forces. Losing trust in the army, they instead began to build up monoethnic militias in areas inhabited by the Dinka, southern Sudan's largest ethnic group, and that to which Kiir belongs. These militias were drawn from the *gelweng*, the pastoralist cattle guards that protect the Dinka's prized livestock.

The SPLM had already attempted to transform the *gelweng* into auxiliary troops during the Sudanese civil war. After the signing of the 2005 agreement, this process intensified. Guns flowed into communities, and everyday life became militarized. Politicians encouraged their constituencies to think of politics in explicitly communitarian terms, with government positions treated as sinecures to be fought over. Soon southern Sudan's fighting forces were almost entirely organized along ethnic lines, as other groups mirrored the SPLM's arming of the *gelweng*. When South Sudan's own civil war broke out in 2013, it initially pitted the Nuer forces that had been absorbed into the SPLA against the Dinka ethnic militias the SPLM had raised, but soon became a broader ethnic conflagration. The civil war ended in 2018 with the signing of a peace agreement—but it did not change the nature of military organization in the country.

The agreement had as its central plank an SSR process designed to bring the belligerent parties together and forge a single national army. Yet after the agreement was signed, the opposite happened: the number of militias multiplied. Kiir, by then South Sudan's president, followed Bashir's playbook and outsourced the country's fighting capacity to local militia groups with more legitimacy on the ground than a regime in Juba concerned only with distributing oil revenues to a narrow coterie of elites. Such militias also offer Kiir deniability: he can claim to be adhering to the terms of the peace agreement because the government can disavow the very militia campaigns it bankrolls, chalking them up to intercommunal fighting.

At the same time, the government is all too willing to be an enthusiastic participant in the theater of SSR, which it turns into a political tool. The government supports the garrisoning of opposition soldiers in cantonment sites, but rather than paying them wages and providing them with food, it starves them while they await an integration into the national army that will never arrive. Their commanders then prove easy pickings for Kiir's regime, which uses its petrodollars to pay them to defect and form new militia forces, further dividing the opposition. The state multiplies militias as a means of maintaining control in the center by fracturing the peripheries of the country.

THROUGHOUT the Horn of Africa, the Weberian dreams of SSR processes have run up against the reality of rule by militia and been chastened. In Somalia, Siad Barre presided over what Alex de Waal has called a "rentier kleptocracy," a government dependent on distributing external flows—foreign military assistance and concessionary loans—to army commanders and militia leaders who established their own provincial fiefdoms. A system of violent armed actors supported by the state—in other words, a militia system—already existed before Barre was overthrown in 1991. The collapse of his regime simply revealed the lineaments of the system more clearly.

Today, despite having received over a billion dollars of international financial assistance and training, the national army is ill equipped and poorly motivated. Officially, it numbers some twenty-seven thousand troops, but just as in Sudan and South Sudan, a good number of these soldiers are ghosts—invented so their all-too-real commanding officers can draw spectral salaries.

If one were to only read SSR documents, one might think the Somali army is a national, unified force. The UN Development Programme, for instance, claims that "Somali federal security institutions have increased professional capacity to exercise political and civilian oversight, deliver security services and coordinate the federal approach to security in accordance with their mandates and in compliance with human rights standards." Underneath the verbiage, the Somali army is a collection of militias playing masquerade. The army almost totally collapsed in 2009 during conflict with al-Shabaab, the militant Islamist group that vies for control of the country with the weak Transitional Federal Government (TFG) in Mogadishu, which is propped up by peacekeepers and the international community. After the army's near collapse, the TFG tried to resuscitate it by carrying out a recruitment drive organized by clan in an attempt to incorporate militias within the army. In clashes with al-Shabaab, the army's only effective fighting forces are militias loyal to local leaders.

Faced with the failure of the SSR process in Somalia, the TFG's international backers—including the United States, Kenya, and Ethiopia, all of which have military forces inside the country—are discussing direct financial support for militia groups, abandoning their decadeslong state-building project. The project, predicated on external backing and counterterrorism funds from foreign powers, has little to show for the billions that have been spent: its main product is a cartel-government constituted by rivalrous politicians competing for payouts from international donors. Somalia is, in effect, a theater-state, staged for the benefit of the international community, which depends on buying the loyalty of militia commanders for its continued survival.

Iraq's state has better internalized the logic of rule by militia, but only by becoming entirely dominated by it. Thanks to a UN sanctions program (1990–2003), Iraq saw an 87 percent drop in per capita income from 1989 to 1996 that led to the breaking up of state institutions. Hussein—just like Bashir—coup-proofed his regime by multiplying the security services and by placing power in informal networks and militia forces like Jaysh al-Quds and

Fedayeen Saddam. The U.S. invasion in 2003 only supercharged a process already well underway.

Since the U.S. decision to disband the Iraqi army in 2003, formal state forces, to the extent they exist, have been intertwined with militias, organized by locality, religious affiliation, or ethnic identity. Despite their claims to be building an Iraqi state through an SSR process, and $25 billion spent training and supplying a new Iraqi national army, the U.S. occupying force enabled militia governance, empowering Sunni *Sahwa* groups during the famous "surge" that had been fighting the United States only a year earlier. As power in Iraq fragmented following the invasion, the United States tried to play the militias off against each other; but just as often, it was being played, with militia forces obtaining materiel and resources on the occupier's dime.

Today, Iraq's security forces are a complicated mixture of armed groups, many of them officially integrated within the government but substantively independent of any meaningful overall authority. As in Somalia, the formalization of the militias within the security forces has laid bare the fiction of a unified government. In its place stands a series of constituencies, political leaders, and military forces, embedded in the formal structures of the state but not beholden to it. One cannot say that the wide variety of armed actors that make up Iraq's Popular Mobilization Units (PMU)—including the Iranian-backed *fasa'il* forces—are separate from the state. Instead, they are a constituent part of it: the formalization of these forces as the PMU gave them access to state funds and patronage. Rather than being a step to creating a national army, the U.S.-led SSR process cemented rule by militia inside the structure of the state.

THOUGH MILITIAS in places like Iraq and Somalia are now part of the state security apparatus, their members are not simply salaried employees but political-economic actors in their own right. The second key characteristic of the contemporary militia is thus that it exists—much like the mercantile companies of seventeenth- and eighteenth-century Europe—as a military force, political organ, and business all at the same time. After its founding in 2013, Hemedti rapidly turned the Sudan's RSF into a multinational firm, following the path taken by Bashir's other security organs; the Sudanese army and the national security service are as much economic empires as fighting forces. Their control of real estate, banking, and commercial services ensures their autonomy from the state.

Gold enabled the RSF's transformation. Following South Sudan's independence in 2011, Sudan lost 75 percent of its oil revenue, as the fields that the Nuer militias had protected all lay in the south. Without petrodollars to grease its wheels, Bashir feared, the patronage system he relied upon to purchase political loyalty would seize up. He urgently tried to reorient the Sudanese economy, and, from 2011 to 2014, the country experienced a gold rush. While Bashir's government had initially envisioned gold mining as an efficiently organized enclave industry, a lack of state capacity instead led to widespread artisanal mining (the term lends a misleading sense of artistry to dangerous forms of extraction). Unlike oil production, artisanal gold mining tends to require a large security force to discipline labor and guard mines. The RSF was just such a force. In 2017 Hemedti took control of the Jebel Amer mine and established a series of holding companies to send the gold to the United Arab Emirates (UAE). These firms enabled him to make a fortune by controlling the purchase and export of gold, outside the ambit of the state. The opacity of the RSF's business operations mirror those of global commodity trading more broadly; the gold from Darfur disappears into an international system that, even if it is often interested in tracing finished goods, is deeply uninterested in making visible the violent labor relations that make global trade possible.

Contemporary militia violence is bound up with new forms of commodity production and new global relations of inequality, and it is often centered on contentions over the circulation of goods. In January last year, clashes between government forces and opposition militias affiliated to the Union for Peace (UPC) in CAR focused on two key nodes: the Béloko customs post, on the way to Cameroon, and the Vakaga prefecture, where UPC forces had once taxed artisanal miners. In the eastern parts of the Democratic Republic of Congo (DRC), conflict between a Rwanda-backed collection of militias, the M23, and the Congolese army (which outsources fighting to militias and private security companies), allows an emergent class of commanders and politicians to profit from the militarization of capital accumulation thanks to taxes at checkpoints and diversions of humanitarian aid.

Yet despite the imaginations of some American NGOs, clashes between militias over sites of resource extraction and nodes in global transport systems do not mean that rule by militia can simply be reduced to a tale of greedy Africans terrorizing local populations and battling for resources. The relationship between the rise of the militias and resource extraction is more complicated than a story of nefarious warlords selling "blood diamonds." Such a narrative appeals to those who hope for conflict-free, guilt-free diamonds for Western consumers, but it leaves intact Central Africa's subsidiary position in the global economy as a mere provider of raw materials. It also occludes the role of global commodity markets, which have obscurity built into them, in enabling militia economies. A U.S. Government Accountability Office review of conflict minerals (which include tin, tungsten, tantalum, and gold) from 2022 determined that half the companies surveyed couldn't determine where the minerals they used came from, *at all.*

The militia economy, furthermore, does not simply—or even primarily—happen at the point of extraction. It grasps hold not of the mode of production but of nodes in global supply chains. Schouten's analysis of the collapse of the infrastructural state in what is now DRC is a good example of how militia economies function. After Mobutu Sese Seko came to power in a coup in 1965, he used high copper prices to expand social services while embarking on nation-building exercises. By the late 1970s and early 1980s, DRC (then Zaire) experienced an enormous economic contraction brought about by a collapse in global commodity prices, state withdrawal from the maintenance of transport routes, and a ruling class that consolidated itself through international loans, the acquisition of mineral rights, and the appropriation of state assets. Massive capital flight ensued—with the acquiescence of international financial institutions.

In response, Mobutu changed course and liberalized mining, speeding up the growth of the artisanal mining sector, which was flooded with young people without the prospect of gainful employment elsewhere. Mobutu also multiplied his security services in an effort to coup-proof his regime, while fragmenting the country along ethnic lines. This fragmentation continued into the 1980s, as the country struggled under an IMF structural adjustment program. Meanwhile the number of roadblocks drastically increased, as impoverished state officials, militia leaders, and communities all intensified forms of predatory activity, taxing the movement of people and goods in the absence of other means of getting by. Checkpoints sprung up along the pathways of international commerce, with coltan and diamonds replacing the ivory of the nineteenth century.

Along these deregulated supply chains emerge new possibilities for militias. In the DRC, some militias have run lucrative schemes looting minerals. Others have even briefly established mining companies of their own, issuing paperwork with all the weight of the state. Yet these groups are outliers. The militias' economic model is centrally based on the control of circulation, not of productive capacity: like the colonialists of old, they have seized the mode of predation. The Rwanda-backed M23 makes its money not in mining but at checkpoints; the former genocidaires of the Democratic Forces for the Liberation of Rwanda (FDLR) branched into businesses both legal and illegal after they fled to the DRC.

For all their differences, the places in which rule by militia has taken hold tend to have remarkably similar class structures. In all the countries surveyed here, a rentier elite calls the shots. This elite has external sources of income: the taxing of resources (oil, gold, coltan) heading to global commodity markets, inflows from international institutions (such as humanitarian aid), and investments from foreign powers (for counterterrorism, peacekeeping, and policing). Such elites depend not on popular legitimacy but on international support. In South Sudan, DRC, and Somalia, among other countries, there is no developmental state. There is rather a theater-state, formally required by the international system, but fundamentally uninterested in providing services and accountability to the population it controls. Instead, the state proves a source of lucrative contracts with external actors, which enable embezzlement by the elite. Rule by militia empowers this fractious elite to sit atop fragmented nation-states, setting local and ethnic groups against each other while profiting from international largesse.

A different mode of predation prevails below. The implosion of the DRC, Sudan, and other countries has created an enormous class of surplus young women and men unable to find a productive place within moribund economies. Decades of war in these countries have produced their own dynamic: widespread dispossession, the destruction of agriculture, and an enormous wealth transfer to the rentier elite that has made peasant and pastoralist forms of life untenable just as more and more young people have come of age. For my friends in South Sudan, if they are not lucky enough to find a job with a humanitarian agency, joining a militia is one of the few life paths open to them. A viable existence might be possible, at least for a while, by taking up work at a checkpoint, taxing, looting, and raiding civilian populations. Often in South Sudan, young men will join local defense forces that rebel against the rentier class that displaces their communities and loots their villages, but these forces' subsidiary positions in the country's political economy means that they can easily be instrumentalized by the very same elite and set against other communities.

This surplus of young people is the third key ingredient in the rise of the contemporary militia. As one can observe in the DRC, the militarization of everyday life has generalized the militia form. Either as a defensive gesture or to acquire scarce resources, communities now set up their own roadblocks to tax trade. Everyone becomes a militia member.

EXTERNAL POWERS can easily intervene in such fragmented environments. In Somalia militias are backed by the UAE and Qatar; in Libya by Turkey, Qatar, Russia, and France, among others; and in Sudan by the UAE, Russia, Turkey, and Iran. But rule by militia is a law for only part of the world. Within the nation-state system, as Amitav Ghosh once suggested, there are increasingly two classes of country. In one class, borders are believed in, the state promises to offer at least a vestige of security, and governments have the capacity to act relatively autonomously from the ethnic and economic forces that constitute them. In the other class of country, the state is a fiction insisted upon by the international community. State-building efforts in these countries have only led to more power being vested in rentier elites, dependent on resources from elsewhere, who have fractured the nations over which they rule.

Recent militia attempts to overturn this order and take power for themselves reveal its emptiness. The Sudanese army wants to portray the RSF as a group of mercenaries intent on looting the state and amassing wealth. But such routinized looting is simply the actuality of the Sudanese state since the 1980s. Rule by militia is the logical consequence of the theater-states that have been propped up by the international community over the last thirty years. In Libya, there is an emergent new order after a decade of civil war: a set of rivalrous militias, backed by different international actors, that have decided it is more profitable to share the spoils of the state than to fight another civil war. Rather than simply appointing politicians to positions while ruling from the shadows, they are now taking an active role in determining the affairs of the state.

In Sudan, as elsewhere, it is sometimes tempting to paint these militias in a heroic light—to see them as the only forces that are attempting to resist the rentier elite despoiling the country. Yet the RSF has no plan for governance in Sudan. Its political strategy is simply the mirror image of its former patrons in the security services: it wishes to *be* the rentier elite, not transform the system.

Rule by militia has not emerged due to the failures of the Iraqi or Sudanese people. Quite the contrary: it is the international economic order and the fiction of the nation-state system that is propping up the rentier elite, enabling militias' seizing of power, and cementing the emergence of two classes of nation-state.

Changing this dynamic is not easy. What is certain is that the liberal dream of a Weberian state will offer no solutions; the theater of state-building has clearly run its course. Any alternative would need to attend to the supply chains and international commodity markets that enable rule by militia. If international actors were actually interested in more democratic forms of governance in places like Sudan, they would address themselves to the growing debt crisis that threatens to further cripple capacity in the Global South. Rather than propping up fictional governments, the international community could focus on the real motor of militia membership: a growing surplus of young women and men thrown off by the global economy which cannot be absorbed by the countries they live in unless massive economic transformations take place at a planetary scale.

SOUTH AFRICA'S ENDURING UNFREEDOM

S'bu Zikode interviewed by Richard Pithouse

APRIL 27 of this year marked thirty years since the formal end of apartheid in South Africa. For the country's newly liberated, Nelson Mandela's 1994 ascension to the presidency was the beginning of a time of great promise. Yet the decades since the African National Congress (ANC) rose to governmental power have, for some, been marked by increasingly bitter disappointment—including for the millions of impoverished people living in shanty towns on the outskirts of cities. In this interview, S'bu Zikode, the president of Abahlali baseMjondolo (Zulu for "Residents of the Shacks"), reflects on what the movement describes as the enduring "unfreedom" that has followed apartheid's end.

Abahlali baseMjondolo emerged in 2005 after a political rupture with the ruling ANC in the Kennedy Road shack settlement, a shanty town near a municipal dump in the port city of Durban that, at the time, housed around six thousand people. After the ANC's brutal suppression of a protest against the sale of land, Zikode and other

Kennedy Road residents joined eleven other settlements to form an autonomous movement. Today Abahlali baseMjondolo has more than 120,000 members in four of South Africa's nine provinces—by far the largest popular movement to have emerged after apartheid. Its repertoire of struggle includes occupations, road blockades, legal forms of mass protest, strategic use of the courts, engagement with the media, and negotiation, all while undergoing a constant process of collective reflection and political education.

In spite of the waves of political violence that have targeted its leaders, the movement has won land for many thousands of people, forced important policy changes, developed an inclusive alternative to the ethnic and xenophobic forms of politics that now fester in South Africa, and enabled access to voice and power in a range of spaces for the country's impoverished people. In our conversation, Zikode speaks about the development of his political consciousness, the movement's decades of struggle, and the need to build a "new system" beyond the existing order.

—Richard Pithouse

Richard Pithouse: You finished school in 1996, two years after Mandela became president. That was still a time of real optimism for many people. What was it like for you?

S'bu Zikode: I felt the world was changing. I wanted to go to university and become a lawyer, so I was excited when I got a letter of acceptance from the university. But then I had to face the real world. I had to travel to Durban [where the university was located]; I needed a place to stay, food, books. Most of all, I needed to pay the university fees. It really stressed me. I felt alone. Luckily, my brother-in-law offered me a place to stay in Durban. When I took the bus to the university from his flat we would pass Kennedy Road [a large shack settlement in Durban].

Even though I had a place to live, I still couldn't find the money for school fees. Then my brother-in-law moved to Johannesburg—meaning that I had no place to stay. It all just got cut. This happened to many Black people. People at home had hopes in me, but I saw myself as a failure. I was thinking more and more about committing suicide. I asked myself why I thought in the first place that I could go to university: I felt that I should have known from the onset that it wasn't for somebody like me. Out of a home and out of money, I moved to Kennedy Road, the settlement I used to pass every day on the bus, and found a job at a petrol station. Accepting that I had been defeated, giving up on my hope of going to the university, and moving to Kennedy Road liberated me from the extreme stress that I was suffering.

RP: This is when you became politically active in Kennedy Road.

SZ: Growing up, I thought that I knew what it was to be poor, but when I got to Kennedy Road, I came to realize that I was not as poor as I thought I was. In that way, setting foot in Kennedy Road was devastating. When a normal person sees children eating worms at the toilet to feed themselves, a child being bitten on the head by a rat, a baby burnt in a fire, or people being brutalized by the police, they want to do something about it. So I got involved in the ANC and was elected as the deputy chairperson of the ward.

But going to the ANC meetings at night really discouraged me. The meetings were dominated by middle-class people, people living in big houses. Meetings could finish at eleven or twelve o'clock at night, and none of the middle-class people there thought to offer us lifts back to the shacks in their cars. I was carrying a mandate from the people who had elected me in Kennedy Road, but there was no interest in the lives of the poor. The meetings were about positions and power: Who do we put in power? Who do we mobilize against?

In 2004 there was a big meeting about a proposed housing development in Kennedy Road with various government departments. The Kennedy Road ANC branch was not invited. Eventually, we learned why: the meeting opposed the housing development. The government officials at the meeting didn't want us to live with middle-class people. They wanted to take us to human dumping grounds far outside the city, even further out than the townships built under apartheid. After this experience, I left the ANC. At the same time, the Kennedy Road Development Committee [an elected group formed to advocate for the shack settlement] declared 2005 as the year of action.

RP: 2004 was a politically explosive year across the country: people, mostly people living in shacks, started organizing road blockades as a form of protest.

SZ: Yes, I remember when Tebogo Mkhonza was killed when police opened fire at four thousand people blockading a major highway in the Free State. He was seventeen. We saw many protests in the media, but we had no connection to what was happening elsewhere in the country.

Then suddenly in March 2005, without explanation, a small piece of land near Kennedy Road that had been promised to us for housing was put under construction. The people working there told us that it had been bought by a businessman who was going to build a brick factory. On March 19, we blocked the road to demand that the ward councilor come and meet with us to explain what was going on. We wanted to talk, but he sent the police to beat us instead. When the councilor finally arrived in an armored police vehicle, he declared that we were criminals and that we must be arrested. The response to our demand to be included in discussions about our own lives was to be treated as criminals.

After we organized the road blockade, we began to meet with other nearby settlements. On October 6, 2005, at a meeting of leaders from twelve settlements, we decided to form one organization, Abahlali baseMjondolo. Our demands for land and housing in the city were clear, and at least understood even if opposed. But we also insisted on being recognized as people who—like all other people—think, as people who should be included in discussions and decision-making, as people who should not be treated like children or criminals, as people whose dignity should be respected.

It was clear that the existing forms of politics at that time ex-cluded the poor. Neither the national government nor any of the city councils wanted to collaborate with the poor to resolve the problems of the poor. No political party represented the poor. The trade unions represented their members, not the millions of poor people outside of formal employment. We needed our own politics: a politics by and for the poor. This politics would be a space for the poor to think together, build our power together, and express and advance our interests. For it to work, we needed our politics to make sense to the masses of the country. The thinking was already there in shack settlements and rural villages, the places where poor communities live, but to build power, that thinking had to be organized, focused, and connected.

RP: The response from the ANC and the local government to the emergence of a movement outside of their control was intensely hostile. You were specifically targeted.

SZ: On September 12, 2006, Abahlali deputy president Philani Zungu and I were arrested on our way to speak on a radio station. We had been warned by a senior politician not to speak to the media. After being arrested, I was beaten by the head of the police station near Kennedy Road. While my head was being banged on the wall, I was constantly asked, Who the hell do I think I am to think I can lead ignorant people, rubbish people, to think that we have a right to live with middle-class people, to be a part of society? The officer asked me if I thought I was a Jesus Christ that could liberate all those *jondolos* [shack dwellers].

When you are being beaten, the physical pain is one thing. But it is also an emotional assault. The inner pain, the inner damage—I found it very stressful. There was so much hatred, when all we were asking for is that the dignity of everyone be respected, for us all to be human beings among other human beings. That one was difficult to heal from because it leads to depression. You go off, you go mad.

That night in the cells, I ask myself, "Who the hell am I?" I wonder who is ordering the police to do this. I ask myself if I should continue with the struggle. Then comes the dawn. I haven't slept. I'm on my own, separated from the people who have asked me to lead, who have given me that responsibility that the police violated. Suddenly I see myself as worthless, infected, a disaster, a disgrace. I am reduced to weightlessness.

But then in the morning, I was brought to appear in court, and I saw that there were so many people in red shirts [the color of the Abahlali baseMjondolo movement] outside in the corridors. When I came up the stairs into the dock, there were so many. Everyone was quiet, but I felt the power of all the people there. I made the decision then to commit my life to this struggle.

Solidarity must be expressed at a personal level. You need to know that you are not alone. People can collapse when they are alone. You see the end of everything. It causes irreparable damage.

RP: The charges were eventually dropped, and the police were successfully sued for torture. But the repression continued.

SZ: Yes—and it got worse. In 2006, there were national municipal elections. In Abahlali baseMjondolo, we followed the position the

LPM [Landless People's Movement] in Johannesburg had taken in 2004, when they said "No Land! No Vote!" and boycotted the election. The LPM were repressed and some of their people were tortured. In 2006, we too declared "No Land! No House! No Vote!" This wasn't just taken as criminal. The politicians spoke as if it were treason. In 2007 we organized a collective march on the Durban mayor, a combined action by all the branches in the different settlements. It was illegally banned. When we decided to march in defiance of the ban, the police attacked us with batons, stun grenades, rubber bullets, and live ammunition. We were treated as not worthy of being human.

RP: The insistence on dignity has always been central to your struggle, and to the struggles of impoverished people around the country, and around the world too.

SZ: A lot of people think that we can only come together around our living conditions. Of course, this is important, and we struggle very hard to improve those conditions. But when we are together, the first thing we must do is recognize the humanity of each and every one of us, because it's only from that position of humanity that we can take our place among other people on this earth. We came to realize why people lie to us and make fake promises to us: it is because in their eyes we are not human enough. It is very deep. So we come together because our humanity is troubled. We come together to develop and defend our humanity, our dignity, to make the world more human. Only after this do questions of living conditions come into being.

For us, the first questions are whether you respect us and how you respect us. Do you engage with us in a respectful way, allow us to speak what we think is right? We want to fully participate in decision-making. We want to participate in development. We want the state and the NGOs to think with us, not for us.

I often talk about the African idea of *ubuntu*. When I do, I'm not just referring to a concept, but the praxis that demonstrates, builds, and defends collective humanity. It is a broad political spirit of humanism that also appeals to the questions of freedom and liberation. And for us, the political form that humanism must take is socialism—particularly democratic socialism built from below.

RP: In 2008 impoverished people, often encouraged by local elites, began to turn on one another. You had been warning for years that the anger of the poor can go in many directions.

SZ: Migrants from other African countries and Asia were attacked and killed in broad daylight, starting in Johannesburg and then elsewhere across the country. We were able to make sure that there were no attacks in any of the areas where we were strong and to give shelter to people who had fled their homes. But once the urgency of the immediate crisis was over, these attacks presented us with a moment of introspection. We realized that we needed to reflect on the things we said, on the commitments we made, and on the contributions we made to society. We had to be clear that we were not only struggling for ourselves to have better lives but to build a better society for everyone.

When oppressed people feel disrespected, they may try to regain some sense of respect by turning on other oppressed people, aiming to make themselves feel better than other people. Since Abahlali baseMjondolo's founding, we had been talking about dignity for ourselves, but in 2008 we had to affirm that we mean dignity for everyone. We declared that a person is a person wherever they may find themselves, no matter where they were born. There is no real freedom without others being free, without your neighbors being free.

We also saw how xenophobia and ethnic divisions are intentionally used to divide poor people—people who might otherwise feel themselves to be the same—when they pose a danger to the system. From time to time, the system has to remind them that they are not the same, that they must see each other as enemies. The system must make poor people think that they are denying each other opportunities to a flourishing life. We must be divided by language, gender, sexuality. But this hate will keep us all poor. And because this hate always weakens the poor, it has to be rejected by poor people first. We have to continue to build our consciousness, to connect with struggles around the world, to learn from each other.

RP: The movement's tenacity eventually forced the ANC to concede your right to participate in the formal political sphere. But as it did so, it shifted repression toward informal violence: violence backed by the police but not carried out by them. This began with an attack by an armed ANC-aligned mob.

Zikode & Pithouse

SZ: We were attacked in the Kennedy Road settlement in late September 2009. At the time, we were having a youth camp at the hall in Kennedy Road. We also had a concert in the community hall, and there was a soccer tournament at the sports ground. A lot was happening.

Our leaders and Xhosa-speaking people living in the settlement were attacked by a large group of men. They were armed, and drunk. They were shouting that they were ANC and Zulu and that S'bu Zikode was putting Xhosa-speaking people ahead of Zulu-speaking people. Homes were ransacked and set alight. The attack continued in broad daylight, in front of the police. That same day, very senior ANC politicians and ministers came to Kennedy Road and announced that Abahlali was disbanded. Later, they went to parliament and said that "Kennedy Road has been liberated."

As a result, we had to go underground. We were scattered all over the place. At first we met secretly in a funeral parlor; then we started meeting openly in a park. We had suffered a heavy blow, but our movement had survived the attack. But then the ANC began to use assassinations. On June 26, 2013, they assassinated Nkululeko Gwala, a leader in our movement, in Cato Crest [an area in Durban that includes public housing, suburban housing, and shack settlements].

RP: You gave an electric speech at Nkululeko's funeral that was widely covered in the Zulu media.

SZ: The funeral, held at Nkululeko's home village in Inchanga, was incredibly tense. From the very start, the ANC tried to make it an

ANC funeral. Imagine that: they can kill you, and then offer to bury you and pay for your funeral.

James Nxumalo, the ANC mayor at that time, was present, along with other high-profile government people, lots of police, and intelligence. After Nxumalo spoke, the senior leaders of the movement took me to the side and counseled me not to speak. It was too dangerous. But then the master of ceremonies, appointed by the Gwala family, called me to speak. Nkululeko was beloved by the community. We could not show fear. And anyway, I was fuming, not scared—just really angry at the situation, at the ANC's lies and hypocrisy.

I spoke very diplomatically, saying, very respectfully, that the family needed and deserved to know the truth. I deliberately went against every single thing that the councilor had said. I explained how we knew Nkulukeko, how we understood him, and what he meant to the community and the movement. I explained that people in rural communities like this village had been abandoned, just like poor people in the cities, and that Nkululeko had given his life for those people, for the oppressed.

I pointed out how many Abahlali members were there to honor their leader, and that we were there to tell the truth about how he was killed. I explained that Nkululeko was killed for his bravery and honesty. I made it clear that senior ANC politicians had publicly threatened him, and that now there were ANC politicians at the funeral wanting to make it an ANC funeral. Emotions were very high. After my speech, the ANC people, including the mayor, could not proceed to speak. The councilor disappeared. It was clear that the ANC were no longer welcome. Immediately after the speech, my

Zikode & Pithouse

comrades pulled me out and put me in a car to rush me out of the village. They felt I was in danger, that it would not be safe to proceed to the grave. But the rest of our members stayed, and it became an Abahlali funeral.

When you have to speak for people, you have to do justice to the people. You to make sure that you say everything that they would have said. It is not about you. I had to satisfy them without fear for myself. After I spoke I was at peace, confident that I had represented the emotions of our members.

RP: Nkululeko's assassination was the beginning of a wave of killings of Abahlali members. Later that year, police killed Nkosinathi Mngomezulu and Nqobile Nzuzua in Cato Crest. Then they assassinated Thuli Ndlovu in 2014, S'bonelo Mpeku in 2017, and S'fiso Ngcobo in 2018—all leaders in the movement. There were others too. In 2016 two ANC councilors were convicted of the murder of Thuli. This seemed to be a turning point in getting the media, human rights organizations, and so on to understand what was happening.

SZ: When poor Black people talk about the repression we face, we are not believed unless the courts, or middle-class people like journalists or academics, confirm the truth of what we are saying. The ANC should be using the power of the people to confront the colonial system that continues to terrorize us and vandalize our humanity. Instead, they are using violence to repress the people so that they can benefit from the system. Some people in the ANC feel that for them to be in charge, for them to be leaders, their power must be felt in a physical way: somebody must feel the pinch; there must be fear. This makes them feel better. It stops them from looking at their emptiness. But fear is not respect. There has to be a new kind of politics, a human form of politics.

RP: You often speak about this kind of politics—becoming human and gaining humanity—as a process.

SZ: The fact that your bones are those of a biological human only means that you have the skeleton of a person. It does not confirm your humanity. You may be a skeleton that is still in the process of building, that still needs *ubuntu* toward yourself, to others, to nature. A human being is incomplete if it is defined in isolation to others.

There is no emancipatory politics without listening to others. Some people will say it's a skill. But listening is much deeper than that. It's about being human, being human together. It's an acknowledgement, an embrace of others. And it's not just an embrace of others as you see them, but an embrace of how they come through the world to this moment, their suffering, their hopes, their views, how they breathe, and how they express themselves.

As a leader, you have to listen to people very carefully. You have to learn from them. Every time you listen to another person you have the opportunity to learn from them. Every person is a world on their own. You can't say that you are on the side of the people, that you are with the people, if you don't take them seriously as people with ideas of their own. We build our humanity through listening.

RP: In 2018 you had to go underground again.

SZ: When you know that a decision has been made to have you killed, you have to consider a lot. I had to remember that it was not about me, and that I had the responsibility to protect people around me: my family and other young leaders. But going underground on your own creates a big problem: self-isolation. Sometimes, that felt like a bigger problem than the problem that forced me underground. The need to go underground to stay alive and to keep people around me safe captured me and put me into a different planet. Psychologically and spiritually, I was removed from the earth.

But in October, Abahlali led a huge march on the Durban City Hall in protest against repression. There were thousands of people there, and many other organizations supported the march including street traders, people living in the old workers' hostels, trade unions, and migrant groups. There were simultaneous solidarity actions in other cities: Johannesburg, Cape Town, London, and New York. There was a clear and powerful demand to end political repression. The movement, working with our comrades in other organizations and other parts of the world, won the space for me to return, and for some time the assassinations stopped.

This kind of repression is always a lesson. It is meant to tell us to know our place, and that we should have always known our place. It is meant to teach us that there are limits to what you can say, what you can enjoy, who you can talk to, what you can demand, what value you can give to your life and to the lives of those around you. If you make the mistake of thinking that you are a human being and that you can engage others as human beings—well, then violence is inevitable.

RP: The loss of four comrades in 2022, three assassinated and one murdered by the police, firmed many Abahlali members' resolve to go from organizing outside the ANC toward actively trying to remove the ANC from power. At the same time, the growing strength of the movement generated a sense that while its power should continue to be based and built in the occupations, the state could not be permanently ceded to oppressive forces. There is now considerable pressure from your members to enter electoral politics.

SZ: Any individual elected into power is highly likely be co-opted, to be made to join the system. What we have seen with the ANC is that Black people can join the electoral system and give it legitimacy for a few years before people see that it has remained the same. It could be the same if poor people take a place in the system. The system is designed for that.

We have to think about how we put *the people* in power, not individuals. That's the question that we have to be battling with, because any individual is likely to be corrupted and changed by the system. It is now clear that we need to talk about the destruction of the capitalist system so that there can be a real reconstruction of a system that places the people—and the humanity and dignity of all people—at the center. We need a new system with a new relation to the world, to the earth, and all its people.

This will take courage—the courage to cross the line. Everyone dies eventually, but what's the use of being killed slowly while the meaning you have given to your life, the value that you have given it, rots away? If we do not have an honest conversation about healing, about decolonizing the mind, we will continue to live in this violence, in the politic of blood.

Aerial view of the Israeli West Bank barrier. Image: Shutterstock

THE QUESTION OF PALESTINIAN STATEHOOD
Leila Farsakh

THE QUEST for Palestinian statehood has long been central to the Palestinian national struggle. In 1971 the Palestine Liberation Organization (PLO) declared the creation of a single democratic state in historic Palestine inclusive of Christians, Jews, and Muslims to be its goal and the only just solution to the Israeli-Palestinian conflict. In 1988 it issued the Palestinian Declaration of Independence, which implied that the PLO accepted the two-state solution, just as its chairman, Yasser Arafat, officially recognized Israel. These developments paved the way to the Oslo peace process in 1993. By 2023, the State of Palestine was officially recognized by 139 of 193 member states of the United Nations, which admitted it as a nonmember state in 2012.

Of course, Palestine remains far from independent or sovereign, having suffered under Israeli occupation throughout this whole period. In the thirty years following the signing of the first Oslo Accords, Israel allowed the transfer of over 500,000 Israeli Jewish settlers to the occupied West Bank (including East Jerusalem), built more than half of a planned 712-kilometer separation wall around it, developed hundreds of checkpoints and roadblocks that fragment Palestinian areas into separate population reserves, and launched five wars against the Gaza Strip, which it has kept under siege for over seventeen years. Already in 1999, Edward Said concluded, "the problem is that Palestinian self-determination in a separate state is unworkable." The internationally endorsed two-state solution—indeed the prospects for any viable Palestinian state—were thus undermined even before the brutal attacks of October 7 on Israeli civilians and military personnel.

The ever-growing toll of Israel's ensuing genocidal war on Gaza has only reinforced judgments that the quest for Palestinian statehood has become futile. The failed April 2024 UN Security Council vote on admitting the State of Palestine into the UN as a full member shows the intransigence of Israeli and U.S. objections. As the number of Palestinians killed continues to rise—as of this writing, more than 34,000 have died, while more than 1.7 million have been displaced and much of the population faces the risk of famine—it has become clear that Palestinians need to move beyond the mirage of the two-state solution.

Even before this war, Palestinians have been grappling with the failure of the two-state solution, forcing them to reassess the relationship between statehood and self-determination and imagine a political resolution that goes beyond partition. The war has compelled them to rethink what political liberation might look like and how to articulate an alternative to the present impasse—one that is democratic, viable, and capable of protecting the equal political rights of Palestinians and Jewish Israelis.

EVER SINCE Palestinians were expelled from their land during the 1948 war, they have sought to fulfill their UN-enshrined right of return. The establishment of the PLO by the Arab League in 1964 reaffirmed this right, but its charter did not specify statehood as part of its mission of liberating Palestine from Zionist colonialism. Only with the ascendence of guerrilla groups into the executive committee of the PLO in the aftermath of the 1967 Six-Day War did the Palestinian national movement tie return with self-determination and political liberation with statehood. The Palestinian struggle for self-determination, however, always carried a certain ambiguity about the relationship between national liberation and statehood.

In this regard, the Palestinian national movement was not much different from most anticolonial liberation movements of the twentieth century. The concept of self-determination, internationalized with Vladimir Lenin's defense of people's right to national independence and reframed by Woodrow Wilson's Fourteen Points in 1918, laid the foundation of a world order composed of nation-states; by 1960 it had become the juridical basis for all national quests for political independence from colonial domination. UN Resolution 1514, adopted that year by the UN General Assembly (UNGA), affirmed self-determination as a fundamental human right. It also declared colonialism a "denial of fundamental human rights" and specified that "all people have an inalienable right to complete freedom, the exercise of their sovereignty and the integrity of their national territory." It thus made self-determination synonymous with national territorial sovereignty—that is, with statehood. An international consensus had thereby been formed around the necessity of independent statehood as a first, if not sufficient, step toward political liberation.

But not all anticolonialists agreed. Many considered the right to self-determination as a people's right to define their political future and choose their own political system of government. They maintained that sovereignty is enshrined above all in the people, or nation, rather than in a territorially bound state per se. These antcolonialists understood the pursuit of self-determination as part of a larger project of remaking the world beyond the Westphalian order of sovereign nation-states. They were aware of what revolutionaries from Toussaint Louverture to Frantz Fanon have warned against: that national independence does not guarantee liberation, for it can create new forms of domination.

In the case of Palestinian statehood, the defining moment of 1971 came when the eighth Palestinian National Council (PNC) convention adopted a unanimous resolution calling for "a democratic Palestinian state" that would be set up "in a Palestine liberated from Zionist imperialism," where "all who wish to do so can live in peace with the same rights and obligations." The convention made clear that "Palestinian armed struggle is not a racist or sectarian struggle against the Jews."

This vision emerged in the face of international denial of the Palestinian question—best exemplified in UN Security Council

Resolution 242 of 1967, which acknowledged the right of each state in the region to "live in peace within secure and recognized boundaries" but did not refer to the Palestinians by name. It simply referred to them as refugees in need of a humanitarian solution, thereby denying their national political character as a people with a right to self-determination.

The PLO's state project was thus as much a matter of national self-affirmation as of political actualization. It aimed to assert Palestinian peoplehood, which Zionism sought to eradicate, as much as to articulate a decolonial political future inclusive of all those who live on the land. While many doubted the sincerity of this inclusive vision—and Israel outright rejected it—Palestinian nationalists were clear about opposing Zionism as a racial colonial project of domination rather than rejecting Jews for their identity.

The PLO's diplomatic and legal efforts in this regard came to fruition in 1974 with UNGA Resolution 3236, which affirmed the legitimacy of Palestinian anticolonial struggle and right to "national independence and sovereignty." The UN national assembly then also recognized the PLO as the sole legitimate representative of the Palestinian people and invited it to participate in the work of the General Assembly like any non–member state, such as the Vatican. Meanwhile, the PLO continued to act as a state in exile, with its various political institutions, electoral structures, and economic services, representing and providing for Palestinians in the diaspora as well as for those under Israeli occupation. In 1974 the PNC's twelfth session adopted the Ten Point Program, which specified that the PLO would employ all means "for the liberation of Palestinian land and setting up a patriotic, independent national authority on every part of the Palestine territory that will be liberated" as part of its strategy for the establishment of a democratic Palestinian state.

The adoption of this program meant that the PLO effectively gave up on the idea of remaking the regional and international order of nation-states. It implicitly admitted the international consensus on the partition of Palestine and the framework for peace outlined in UN Resolution 242. Although many Palestinians contested the possibility of a Palestinian state without dismantling Zionism first, the majority accepted that national independence was a first step toward national liberation, even if the content and shape of this state—as well as the extent to which its creation would be the means to, or the end of, decolonization—remained contested.

Linking self-determination with statehood thus gave the Palestinian liberation struggle a concrete political meaning in an international system that bestowed on states the primary responsibility of representing and protecting the human and political rights of citizens. This view gained strength after Israel's war against the PLO in Lebanon in 1982 and the failure of Arab states to come to the rescue of the Palestinians. The PLO's Declaration of Independence in 1988, announced after the outbreak of the First Intifada, represented the official Palestinian acceptance that national self-determination could only be fulfilled on part of historic Palestine—and that it would be attainable by negotiating with, rather than defeating, Israel.

This Palestinian vision of statehood, and its acceptance of the two-state solution, thus became the price of the Palestinian historical compromise with Israel: it was the only way for Palestinians to advocate for themselves at peace negotiations where UNSC Resolution 242 set the terms of any possible resolution to the conflict. A Palestinian state in the West Bank and Gaza, i.e. on only 22 percent of Palestine, was considered better than no state because it promised political independence and would allow a means for the return of refugees, even if it could not restore justice to the Palestinians for the Nakba. Above all, it promised citizenship rights. In other words, the Palestinian state project affirmed the Palestinian "right to have rights," which, as Hannah Arendt explained, is the rationale for, and responsibility of, any claim for statehood.

FOR THE PLO leadership, the Oslo peace process in 1993 provided an opportunity to territorialize these dreams of Palestinian statehood. With the signing of the Declaration of Principles in 1993 and Interim Agreement on the West Bank and Gaza Strip in 1995, the PLO acquiesced to a conflict resolution approach intrinsically tied to territorial partition as a paradigm for achieving a minimum of Palestinian rights. It also accepted Israel's insistence that the starting point of the conflict was the 1967 war, not the 1948 war. Although fully aware that the Oslo process did not end the occupation or specify as its end goal the creation of a Palestinian state, the Palestinian leadership remained committed to proving that Palestinian statehood was both necessary and achievable.

Starting with Arafat's return from Tunis to Gaza in 1994 and his role as the head of a democratically elected Palestinian National

Authority (PNA) in January 1996, the Palestinian official narrative thus shifted from decolonization to state-building. The PNA focused on behaving as a state in order to be recognized as one, embarking on a wide variety of activities that ranged from setting up a new police force and various ministries to devising national development strategies and ritualizing presidential salutes while receiving foreign ambassadors. Such performances of statehood sought to abstract the reality of occupation, not so much in order to deny it but to refuse to be constrained by it. They were attempts, however limited, to affirm Palestinian agency and legitimate national existence despite Israel's continuous obstructions.

The PNA's belief that national independence was attainable through state-building rather than revolutionary armed resistance was best exemplified by the Fayyad technocratic government in 2007. Set up in the aftermath of the international boycott of Hamas's electoral victory in 2006 and the Fatah-Hamas debacle in June 2007, this government defined its mission as providing "the final push to statehood." It worked on proving Palestinian institutional readiness for independent statehood, as advised by PNA's new international sponsors, the World Bank and the International Monetary Fund.

State-building thus became about law and order, not about national unity or democratic representation. It confined the meaning of self-determination to the establishment of a neoliberal state, as defined by Washington's conception of good governance. Its mission was to foster "institution-building" and fiscal transparency in order to ensure the development of a vibrant private sector. It established a kind of statehood that was not sovereign but responsible for the management of Palestinian populations under its control and entitled to political independence in a distant and uncertain future.

Even more assiduously, since 2008 this state-building effort proved to be a site of governance and control—an effort by which the PNA shaped power relations over space and people, rather than a strategy that could effectively halt Israeli settlement construction or end the siege on Gaza. This control was visible at the macro level in the creation of a repressive police force and prison system in the West Bank and Gaza Strip and in the failure to create independent and transparent judiciary. It also was clear at the micro level in the way state-building efforts reshaped access to resources and power, whether in developing the infrastructure for a modern electricity grid and road system or defining the terms of public-private partnerships. Meanwhile, the PNA was unable to challenge the settler colonial reality its state project was embedded in, given that it remained responsible for safeguarding Israeli security. The failure of regional and international powers to exert pressure on Israel to retreat fully from the West Bank and Gaza—or even to adhere to the terms of the Oslo agreements—meant that the Palestinian state was going to be neither independent nor democratic.

Indeed, it is impossible to explain the persistence (and failure) of the Palestinian state project without considering the international investment in it. The Quartet on the Middle East—comprising the UN, European Union, United States, and Russia—has been the major advisor and funder of the Palestinian state project, delivering over $44 billion to the Palestinian territories since 1994. Apart from disbursing some of this money into humanitarian aid, the international community focused on improving the PNA's institutional capability to prove Palestinian readiness for political independence, giving special attention to enhancing the PNA's monopoly over the use of violence in the West Bank and Gaza.

The meaning of statehood has thus been restricted to the power of an internationally recognized authority to impose law and order—crowding out goals such as fostering democratic accountability or ensuring Palestinian unity, let alone adhering to international law or forcing Israel to withdraw from Palestinian land. And by prioritizing Israel's security concerns in delineating the extent of Palestinian territorial and demographic jurisdiction, the international community has largely ignored the importance of territorial contiguity for the viability of any Palestinian state.

The cumulative effect of these developments of the past thirty years has been to transform the Palestinian state project from a vehicle for national liberation into an effort to dissolve the Palestine question altogether. Juridically, Oslo confined the Palestinian nation to the West Bank and Gaza Strip, compromising the unity of the Palestinian people and the political rights of Palestinian refugees abroad. It also undermined the national Palestinian political system with the creation of new territorially truncated political bodies: the PNA and the Palestinian Legislative Council effectively superseded the PLO and its Palestinian National Council, which had historically represented Palestinians both inside and outside the West Bank and Gaza Strip.

The Palestinian project of national self-determination has thus been emptied of emancipatory potential. It was not in vain, however, for it fulfilled an important historical role, serving as the vehicle for affirming Palestinian political existence as a national group with a right to political independence. It helped win legitimacy for the Palestinian struggle of self-determination in the eyes of the international community, which has admitted the State of Palestine into multiple international institutions since 2011. But it proved to be insufficient for political and territorial liberation because it remained confined within a partition paradigm that did not stop, let alone undo, Israeli settler colonialism.

ISRAEL'S LATEST war on Gaza has not only confirmed the reality of Israel's effective sovereignty over Palestine—a reality that has been increasingly described as apartheid. It has also revealed the brutal dimensions of this condition. Palestinians in the Gaza Strip are subjected to carpet bombing and to the annihilation of their educational, health, and housing infrastructure while enduring displacement and famine. Those in the West Bank, meanwhile, continue to live in fragmented population reserves pervaded by Israeli checkpoints while facing mounting settler violence and military incursions; as of this writing, more than 500 have been killed, and thousands have been taken into Israeli custody, since October 8.

Israel's latest war on the Palestinians clearly indicates that the conflict has entered a new phase, even if its settler colonial character has not changed. The premise upon which the conflict has been managed for the past thirty years has been shaken, as Israel can no longer rely on the claim that the conflict is confined to the land occupied in the 1967 war and that a resolution can be achieved through a peace process, or a partition paradigm, that does not end Israel's occupation of Palestinian land. The more foundational question posed in 1948, if not before, has resurfaced and demands still an answer: Who has political rights in the land between the river and the sea, and how are these rights going to be exercised and protected? Can this land accommodate two national groups, and if so, under what political configuration?

Many Palestinian activists and academics have sought to address these questions long before the events of October 7. Over the past two decades, in particular, many have sought to redefine the meaning of political liberation in the wake of the maimed project of a Palestinian nation-state. This alternative discourse identifies settler colonialism, rather than occupation, as the impediment to political independence—and thus views decolonization, rather than partition, as the required path to peace.

One aspect of this work has entailed appeals to Palestinians' inalienable rights. This rights-based approach gained prominence with the rise of the Boycott, Divestment and Sanctions (BDS) movement and the 2004 opinion by the International Court of Justice (ICJ) declaring Israel's separation wall to be illegal. This approach sees in international law a potent tool for holding Israel accountable to its international obligations—as most recently manifested in South Africa's genocide case against Israel at the ICJ. It emphasizes the unity of Palestinian rights, including the right of return, freedom from occupation in the West Bank and Gaza, and the right to equal citizenship for the Palestinians living inside Israel. The BDS move-

Farsakh

ment, meanwhile, has been particularly effective in mobilizing support for new strategies of nonviolent resistance and generating growing international solidarity with Palestinians at the grassroots level and in different policy circles (including academia, local governments, unions, and churches).

The rights-based approach, however, stops short of offering a comprehensive political strategy—one capable of uniting the Palestinian body politic with a viable political alternative to the stalled two-state solution. Proposals to that effect have taken two broad forms.

The first rejects the very idea of a Palestinian state as a political aspiration. It considers the state a site of inherent violence and thus bound to be oppressive, especially in the absence of a free and active civil society. It emphasizes that sovereignty lies with the people, not with the state, and highlights that globalization has undermined the importance of territorial sovereignty. Politically, this approach affirms the political agency of the Palestinians everywhere, not just in the Occupied Territories. It embraces the fragmented and exilic Palestinian experience while providing a resounding rejection of the PNA's attempt to monopolize the Palestinian "we."

The second approach is more skeptical about the possibility of transcending the state as a political project, given that it remains the sovereign guarantor of rights and security. Advocates of this approach seek rather to redefine the content of the state project by rejecting ethnonationalism and deterritorializing the fulfillment of the right to self-determination. They argue that a democratic one-state solution is the only means to decolonize the ongoing apartheid reality. There is no consensus, however, on whether such a state should be a liberal democratic state or a binational one, largely because there is no agreement on how to accommodate the political rights of Jewish Israelis in a decolonized political entity. Binationalists maintain that the collective rights of Jewish citizens would be recognized as equal, not superior, to Palestinian collective rights in a future democratic state. Others argue that a decolonized polity can only protect Jewish individual rights as citizens but not their Zionist national identity, since Zionism is a settler colonial project premised on the destruction of the Palestinians.

Israel's present genocidal onslaught on Gaza has given further credence to this line of argument. Decolonizing Israel, and thus Zionism, is going to be central to any discussion of the one-state solution. Voices calling for it are growing within the Jewish community in the United States and elsewhere and within a new generation of students and activists leading international protests in support of Palestinian rights worldwide. According to Said, it falls on the Palestinians, as unfair as this might sound, to show the way toward liberation, since "no people, for bad or for good, is so freighted with multiple, and yet unreachable or indigestible, significance as the Palestinians. . . . Their relationship to Zionism, and ultimately to political and spiritual Judaism, gives them a formidable burden as interlocutors of the Jews." This war has made it clear that they cannot, and should not, carry this burden alone.

THREE CHEERS FOR THE ADMINISTRATIVE STATE
Janice Fine & Hana Shepherd

AT A RECENT conference, someone brought up the importance of defending "the state" against right-wing ideologues. Outrage ensued—so
much, in fact, that the afternoon session had to be canceled. That
presenter never got the chance to explain that she was *not* talking about
the carceral state, the police, or the military-industrial complex. She
was talking about the need to resist the ongoing commodification of
government services and the sweeping elimination of regulation—in
other words, the right's agenda. Think tanks planning for a second
Trump administration have big plans to dismantle the federal bureaucracy and limit the power of federal agencies to interpret the
intent of the laws they are charged with implementing.

There is a reason the right is laying these plans. Over the past
three and a half years, the Biden administration has demonstrated
just how powerful the actions of the administrative state can be
in the service of labor power and antimonopoly regulation. This
is precisely what the conference presenter had in mind: the work

of transforming the state we have into the state we want—challenging, not defending, the status quo. She probably would have dug herself in even deeper with the audience had she used the word "enforcement," but that's what she was thinking of: the power of the administrative state to implement and enforce labor laws, particularly the innovative worker protection laws like high minimum wage standards and paid sick and safe time that have been enacted by state and local governments.

That presenter was one of us. Simply put, policies must be enforced to be effective. But it is not a given that enforcement is done in a way that can support new labor laws' broad political goals of ending worker exploitation and permanently raising standards in poorly paid and dangerous industries. Even deep-blue cities can have conservative implementation and enforcement practices that hamstring the progressive intent of policies.

As part of our work at the Workplace Justice Lab at Rutgers University, we partner with state and local labor enforcement agencies to provide them with resources and support to strengthen how they do enforcement. We focus in particular on helping them implement what are known as *strategic enforcement* practices, which move away from a reactive, solely complaint-based approach and instead target high-violation sectors using limited enforcement resources carefully and creatively to systematically change employer behavior. We also develop partnerships with worker organizations, who spend years supporting and building trust with workers whose fear of employer retaliation keeps them silent. In our experience, such engagement is essential to reach these vulnerable workers, who often doubt that the government agencies meant to protect their rights will help them, no matter how egregiously those rights have been violated.

From this work, we have learned that staff in labor standards enforcement offices are often excited to adopt new practices to improve their work. But we have also found that few see their mission as realizing the full, transformative promise of progressive laws. They often see their job as following the rules to investigate when a worker complains about their rights being violated, rather than thinking about their job as a mechanism for improving well-being and combating work-related inequity.

BECAUSE NEW federal labor and employment reforms have been blocked for decades, organizers and policy entrepreneurs have pivoted to policy campaigns at the state and local level. Fortunately, they've been very successful. In the last dozen years, the number of cities and counties with minimum wage laws requiring employers to pay all workers above the federal level increased almost twelvefold, from five municipalities to fifty-nine. Twenty-one cities and counties now have paid sick leave laws. Over 150 cities and counties have laws requiring employers to at least consider the applications of those with criminal records. Nine cities and one state (Oregon) have fair scheduling laws, which require large retail employers (and, in some cities, fast food or food service establishments) to provide workers with advanced notice of work schedules, and to pay them if they cancel a shift at short notice. Seattle, Philadelphia, and Washington, D.C. have legislation protecting domestic workers specifically.

With the exception of the minimum wage laws, all these ordinances provide novel standards and protection to workers. They require employers to extend the protections typically provided voluntarily to middle-class workers to low-wage workers, many of whom are Black or foreign-born women, who are unlikely to receive such rights without an external mandate. They are profoundly feminist in their orientation, accounting for the realities of who does work across formal employment and the home and family. Paid sick leave and fair scheduling laws, for example, keep women and other workers with caretaking responsibilities from having to choose between caring for their families and their formal employment.

Crucially, twenty-six municipalities with these new protections also have a government body tasked specifically with enforcing them. Some of these new local agencies also engage in co-enforcement, partnering with worker centers, unions, community organizations, and legal nonprofits, providing education and training, identifying violations, and supporting investigations. This combination—innovative local labor standards policies paired with innovative enforcement—may be our best hope of providing guardrails for today's overwhelmingly nonunion, private sector, low-wage workers. It could also establish a model for negotiating over, and then enforcing, minimum sectoral wage standards at the local level.

Of course, doing so will require actually carrying out the organizing to build power sufficient to compel these negotiations—and doing it *with*, rather than on behalf of, workers. There is already some movement toward local sector-specific minimum employment standards, and local enforcement agencies have the potential to function as the institutional foundation within which new models of organization, representation, and bargaining could be incubated. But agencies' practices are not always aligned with new policies' normative goals.

This is because enforcement does not happen on a tabula rasa. Just as agencies have existing laws and regulations, they also have an embedded mindset of bureaucratic neutrality: the idea that government officials should act as nothing more than impartial arbiters. The roots of this mindset are deep. In his landmark 1887 essay, "The Study of Administration," Woodrow Wilson argued that "administration lies outside the proper sphere of *politics*. Administrative questions are not political questions."

The urban progressive movement that emerged in the late 1880s embraced Wilson's arguments that science, expertise, and management would solve the problems of city life. Its advocates called for professionalizing government through greater regulation, modernizing tax assessment, and building out civil service systems. They were eager to dismantle the power of urban political machines built on working-class power, and so pushed for reducing the number of elective positions and creating new agencies to be run by professionals in their fields. By the late 1890s, reformers had developed a theory of governance built on four pillars: low taxes and strict budgetary control, strict separation between day-to-day administration and politics, administrative expertise, and efficiency. In Grant McConnell's memorable description: "In the high tide of Progressivism confidence in impersonal expertise took on an almost millennial tone."

Camilla Stivers characterized the Progressive movement during this period as having two faces: one that was focused on municipal management and administration, and the other on social justice. The latter face—comprised in part of urban women's clubs and trade union leagues, federations of labor, and the growing Settlement House movement—blamed businesses and the wealthy for worker exploitation and the plight of the poor. And while municipal management and social justice goals initially operated in tandem, over time, they drifted apart from each other. As a result, the existing approach to reform, which prioritized eliminating unfair economic competition, promoting worker voice, improving conditions, and raising wages as a way to make lives better, was devalued in a public administration that privileged procedures and rules over ends.

The effects of this legacy have been profound. With some ebbs and flows along the way, the disconnect between policy goals and implementation has carried through to the present day. Today's bureaucrats assume that they are there to follow rules and procedures, and, to that end, that they should be "neutral" on political matters and abstain from substantive goals—and this limits the effectiveness of their work. Even when local labor standards administrators adopt more effective enforcement practices, they largely do not see their work as a means to achieving the larger goal of raising the standard of living for poor and working-class city dwellers. Of course, adopting more effective practices, like many municipalities have done in recent years, is enormous progress. But that's only part of the equation. If progressives want to shift societal expectations around how businesses should treat their employees, they will need a broader vision of justice underlying their strategies.

To get there, state and local progressives need more than a set of good practices of governance; they need a new mission for governance as well. Without one, administrative staff will fall back on what agencies have always done, hitching backward enforcement regimes to forward-looking policies and thus carrying on the long history of separating policies' intention from their real-world implementation.

WHAT WOULD this governance mission look like? Our experiences and observations have led us to an approach we call *transformative governance*. It requires the integration of three foundational tenets.

First, transformative governance considers policy and the enforcement of that policy as one comprehensive entity, not as separated from each other. As Barry Karl characterized the New Deal mindset (in contrast to the Progressive Era mindset), civil service provided protection from the "mindless victimization produced by partisan politics," but it was not a mechanism for preventing bureaucrats from accomplishing policy outcomes. Instead, in this approach bureaucrats can embrace their role as implementers of a political vision.

Second, transformative governance understands that addressing the structural basis of existing power imbalances in employer-employee relationships is central to the work of government, and can be done while carrying out fair investigations that are decided on their merits. As Julie Su, Acting U.S. Secretary of Labor, argued during her tenure as California Labor Commissioner: "We are not neutral. . . . The fair outcome may very well be decisions that all go one way in favor of workers whose rights are violated."

Third, transformative governance reimagines the goal of administration as realizing the well-being and equity vision of laws. Every labor investigator in the state of California acknowledges this challenge. Emblazoned on each one's business card are these words: "The mission of the California Labor Commissioner's Office is to ensure a just day's pay in every workplace in the State and to promote economic justice through robust enforcement of labor law."

Transformative governance takes a holistic approach to realizing substantive outcomes: equity, dignity, and the protection of those among us who are most vulnerable. It is not about bureaucrats bending to the whims of those in power or attempts to subvert principles of democracy and the rule of law. It requires constant updating as firm and industry structures and strategies morph with respect to employment relations and their impact on workers, especially the women, immigrants, indigenous, and Black and brown workers who experience a higher level of employer violations than others. It requires that regulators base their strategies on addressing the underlying causes of substandard working conditions. In short, this form of governance responds to the embeddedness, as scholar and politician Karl Polanyi would put it, of market and society. It also understands the importance of relationships—both within government and with civil society groups—as a key aspect of recognizing and navigating complexity within administration.

At the Workplace Justice Lab, we meet many labor administrators and investigators who entered the field because of their commitment to economic justice. Many are hungry for a governing practice *and* a mission. When newly elected governors and mayors place people into important administrative leadership positions and staff roles in labor departments, we seek them out and provide support around implementing strategic enforcement practices. At the same time, we challenge them to embrace a systemic orientation toward rooting out labor violations—one that understands labor standards enforcement as a mechanism to redress underlying structural problems in the labor market with the unapologetic goal of permanently raising standards across low-wage, high-violation industries. Most importantly, we support them with the tools they need to manage in the service of this vision. Without them, agencies are likely to default to the way that enforcement has always been done.

Transformative governance is an approach that can be applied to many areas of state and local regulation: public health and health care, economic development, and environmental protection, to name but a few. There is plenty of work to do to make this mission a reality, but that is why we must support, and cheer, the local administrative state.

IS THE STATE HERE TO STAY?

Jonathan S. Blake

IN EARLY 2022 the *Economist* decried "governments' widespread new fondness for interventionism." The state was "becoming bossier" and "more meddlesome," it complained.

In fact, the state's punitive arm was plenty active in the United States and the United Kingdom while neoliberalism was shredding public goods, to say nothing of the foreign interventions of these states over this period. But on the economic front, at least, the *Economist* was right: state spending and regulation are back. The U.S. federal government has recently spent $5 trillion under two presidents to act against public health and economic threats, and the Biden administration is boastfully pursuing industrial policy. Add to this a more aggressive approach to antitrust enforcement and regulation in general, and the administrative and developmental elements of today's American state look very different than they did in 1990 or even 2010.

And it's not just the United States. The COVID-19 pandemic prompted a massive increase in state intervention around the world as governments pumped their economies full of cash and undertook public health measures—"among history's largest exercises in state power," in historian Peter Baldwin's analysis. China's zero-COVID interventions were perhaps the most dramatic example. Xi Jinping has also reversed a three-decade trend toward decentralization, using the state to support allies and key industries, promote an anti-inequality "Common Prosperity" agenda, and crack down on independent sources of power. Russia, for its part, has turned to the state to mobilize the Russian economy and society into a war machine, while the European Union is easing off ordoliberalism to promote a green agenda with carbon tariffs and has even taken steps toward becoming more state-like, issuing common debt for the first time during the pandemic.

In light of these developments, it is perhaps no surprise that the state is the object of renewed scholarly attention. Three recent books demonstrate its place in ongoing debates. In *The State*, philosopher Philip Pettit exhorts political theory to return to classic questions about the nature, scope, and legitimacy of state power. In *The Project-State and Its Rivals*, historian Charles Maier gives a sweeping analysis of one particularly activist form of the modern state. And in *The Life and Death of States*, historian Natasha Wheatley recovers alternatives to prevailing ideas about state sovereignty through the lens of the Habsburg Empire.

Together these works help illuminate the stakes of our new statist age, along with its possible limitations. Renewed control over capital is a welcome development, but can the revitalized state rise to today's challenges?

A MAJOR AIM of Pettit's book is to place the state back at the center of political philosophy. Following the publication of John Rawls's monumental *A Theory of Justice* (1971), he laments, the state took a back seat to debates about justice. He makes a case for linking these concerns, in part, by arguing that the state is necessary for justice. And he further justifies his focus on the state with a dose of "realism": as a political form, he thinks, it is simply "destined to survive"—so it is essential to have a theory of the nature of the state and the function it must play in the lives of citizens.

One element of such a theory asks, just what *is* a state? Pettit offers a functional account. Polities count as states, he argues, when they fulfill the central function of "individually securing its citizens against one another under a regime of law that it safeguards against internal and external dangers." By establishing and enforcing "a coercive, territorial regime of law" and protecting itself from enemies foreign and domestic, the "fully functional state" provides "each citizen a reliable, determinate zone of legal security, however limited it may be, within which they can decide on how they want to live their lives."

This is a fairly minimal view of the state—not exactly resonant, at first blush, with the ambitions of today's neostatists in the Biden administration. It reflects Pettit's career as an interpreter and exponent of "neo-republicanism"—a tradition of political thought that focuses on liberty. As Pettit has developed it, republican liberty is a condition of non-domination, meaning that individuals are not subject to

Blake

unchecked power. To be in a position of non-domination "is just to be in a position where no one can interfere arbitrarily in your affairs," Pettit explains in *Republicanism: A Theory of Freedom and Government* (1997). With *The State*, he provides "a prologue to a neo-republican theory of justice," detailing his vision of the state as the institution capable of nurturing justice and preventing domination.

The functional state that Pettit sketches shies away from extremes and aims for a sense of balance. "Moderation" is one of the book's key words. For Pettit, the moderate state avoids the pitfalls that concern three prominent political approaches. First, despite the fears of Thomas Hobbes and other proponents of an "absolutist form of statism," the state does not necessarily curtail opportunities for its citizens to generate "collective, countervailing power." Second, the anxieties of "radical" libertarians notwithstanding, the state can "recognize and honor" significant individual rights. And third, against the tut-tutting of laissez-faire theorists, the state "will have the capacity to intervene productively in the market economy." Drawing on the empirical work of Karl Polanyi and Katharina Pistor, Pettit argues that since the market economy is not independent from the state (as laissez-faire theorists believe), "modern pressures"—from citizens and financial interests—"would force" any functional state to take interventionist measures.

In other words, Pettit's state—which in the end looks strikingly similar to the modern, liberal state—seeks to steer between the Scylla of a maximal state and the Charybdis of libertarian fantasies. This solution may seem obvious enough, and many would likely embrace it. The most important condition of balance, Pettit maintains, is the "balance of power between rulers and ruled." Any benefits that the state might deliver can only be actualized when "there is a rough balance of power between rulers and their subjects." It is precisely the condition of equipoise that prevents the domination of "decision takers" by "decision makers." This balance of power is so central to Pettit's analysis that without it a polity is not even considered a state; polities that are too powerful or too powerless are actually "failed or failing counterparts." "If they still count as states," Pettit writes, "that is only in the sense in which the heart that has ceased to pump blood is still a heart." On this view, the state is not just a tool for moderation but *constituted* by moderation.

For all this focus on balance within states, however, Pettit pays no heed to balance *among* states. The international system is practically defined by the power of great power "decision makers" over everyone else. Pettit would likely say, correctly, that there isn't a world state, so of course a dog-eat-dog dynamic prevails. But if the domestic decision makers in nearly every polity are ultimately decision takers at the international scale, is the state as he defines it really a major actor in world politics? In fact, even the statehood of the United States is in question on Pettit's account. Examined through the lenses of the power of the wealthy over policy or the power of the police over many communities, the U.S. state—though hegemonic on the global stage—starts to look like a "heart that has ceased to pump." Pettit shies away from such a judgment, but his argument suggests a sense in which Americans might be construed as stateless—or at least members of a "failed or failing counterpart," for whom a significant reconstruction of the polity is in order.

Despite Pettit's attempt to recover a tradition of inquiry that Rawlsian concerns with justice have displaced, *The State* resembles *A Theory of Justice* in focusing on ideal theory; it contains little history or sociology of the state, or politics for that matter. Theoretical arguments may be helpful so far as they go, especially in setting goals and in the work of public reasoning—that is, in justifying state action to citizens. But both state power and the pursuit of justice are ultimately practical matters, and even if we all agreed on the desirability of Pettit's state, we would need a strategy for building it. As Thad Williamson recently put it in these pages, ideal theories of "what a hypothetical good society would look like" generally neglect "the process by which we might get there."

Rather than positing an intrinsic, ahistorical relationship between justice and the state, what can we learn by viewing the pursuit of justice as one of the state's "projects" that emerged over the twentieth century?

MAIER'S BOOK gives us the conceptual language to think about this historical development. He zooms in on the "rise and eclipse" of a particular state form he calls the "project-state," a twentieth-century activist state committed to a "transformative agenda" and "that consciously aspired to inflect the course of history."

For Maier, the category is expansive and morally neutral: it includes New Deal America and Germany under Hitler, the postwar British welfare state and China under Mao's Great Leap Forward.

As Maier puts it, "project-states have served as a force for good and for evil." The defining characteristic of the project-state is that it sought "not merely to govern day to day" but "aspired to change social and economic relations in a profound way." Its raison d'être was "to transform the nonpolitical institutions of society—economic outcomes, public health, religious commitments and secular loyalties, landscapes and cityscapes."

The rise of the project-state ushered in a sea change in political arrangements. For much of the early history of modern states—when monarchies and divine right reigned—there was simply no intellectual or moral framework to suggest it was the state's role, or even within the state's abilities, to improve the lives of the many. This attitude was displaced over the course of the nineteenth century, as Maier (and many others) have charted. Transformations in scientific, social, and political thought introduced both the idea of progress and the idea that the state could intervene to promote progress in society. At the same time, new technologies and administrative techniques created the capacity for the state to act at scale in society. The invention of the railroad, steam-powered boat, and telegraph, Maier argued in a previous book, "let extensive territories be governed . . . in real time: they conveyed the sense that national space was a realm of relatively simultaneous application of control." No longer solely focused on the benefits to the ruling dynasty and in possession of a new intellectual and technological toolkit, nineteenth-century states, observed the sociologist Charles Tilly, "involved themselves much more heavily than before in building social infrastructure, in providing services, in regulating economic activity, in controlling population movements, and in assuring citizens' welfare."

Indeed, many state functions that we now expect—and that are central to Pettit's account—first emerged in this era. Modern policing, including the idea of a dedicated, professional police force, was established in Britain in 1829. Modern government social statistics began to be collected in large quantities in the 1830s and 1840s. Modern public health developed in response to advances in science and medicine, such as Louis Pasteur's discoveries on the germ theory of diseases in the 1850s and John Snow's famous map of the London cholera outbreak in 1854. Modern border controls, including the introduction of the passport, began to be implemented, though borders remained much more porous until the Great War. Bismarck's passage, in 1883, of state-based health insurance for workers in Germany heralded the arrival of the modern welfare state.

These nineteenth-century projects were merely the foothills of the project-states that constitute what Maier calls "the Himalayas of twentieth-century history." The strength of his book is that it situates these towering state-led ambitions to form, inspire, reform, and reinspire a population alongside three additional "protagonists" of history. One is resource empires, which were built to be "cash cows for beneficiaries in the metropole or settlers in place" so that they could "enjoy the fruits of overseas colonies." The other two were territorially unbound "organizations and networks that aspired not to sovereign power but to moral and political influence and/or to material gain"—specifically, transnational domains of governance and of capital.

By governance, Maier means the web of "nonstate or interstate organizations that proposed to intervene in society by invoking ethical, normative, or 'expert' considerations." This network of transnational activists sought to build "a society of values" through an incredible range of institutions: the League of Nations and United Nations; the global envelop of international law and the bevy of organizations such as Human Rights Watch and Amnesty International that seek to hold states to its standards; bodies that promote cross-national technical standards and scientific collaboration such as the International Tele-communication Union, International Science Council, and International Rice Research Institute; and a wide variety of NGOs, from the Ford Foundation to Oxfam to the Konrad-Adenauer-Stiftung. Where Maier takes a neutral view of project-states, he is more positive about governance. "I tend to believe that institutions of governance play a generally beneficial role and deserve the authority they claim," he writes. The point is not totally convincing. If project-states can "construct the Tennessee Valley Authority on one hand and Auschwitz on the other hand," why do we "not usually refer to the governance of the Mafia or the Zetas"? What is the Islamic State if not a transnational organization trying to construct "a society of values"?

The realm of capital certainly made no pretense of its moral commitments. For Maier, it "has included the individuals and or-ganizations—firms, banks, trade associations—that participated in markets, where they reciprocally exchanged goods, labor, real property, and promises of future payments in a framework supposedly free of legal or extralegal coercion." Throughout the book, these economic agents work to increase their profits in a world defined by shifting relations between themselves and the other three protagonists. Much of the narrative charts the actions of the energy industry—first coal, then oil—to secure its place among other political, economic, and ideological forces. These forces, particularly those of the state, were at times energy's staunch ally, but at other times they acted to rein in the sector's power.

This points to Maier's true ambition: to plot "the changing balance among the protagonists of the twentieth century." His history is one of relations. It seeks to explain the structure of world history by charting how project-states, resource empires, governance institutions, and the globalizing web of capital vied for power. Over time, the balance of these forces changed. In the three decades after World War II the project-state "beckoned with a renewed luster" and took on an "expanded role" while "agendas for governance and projects for capital remained overshadowed under state or interstate umbrellas." Yet by the late 1960s and 1970s, capital and governance began to reassert their power over a diminishing national state.

This story of the exhaustion of the postwar political-economic order has now been told many times; what sets Maier's account apart is the way he weaves together the work of capitalist activists and their allies in politics and think tanks with the work of governance activists in the same years. His wide-angle lens shows how the political and economic turbulence of that period led not only to the Volcker shock but to the rising prominence of NGOs and foundations seeking to restore order and stability at home and abroad.

As historian Samuel Moyn has shown, human rights—one node in the web of governance—emerged precisely in the 1970s following the floundering of state-led capitalist, socialist, and nationalist projects. What's more, Moyn argues, it is no accident that the rise of human rights coincided with the rise of economic inequality. The projects to roll back the state's use of fiscal authority and regulation and to roll back the state's use of torture and political imprisonment shared similar impulses and dynamics. At several points, Maier argues that neoliberal rollback of the postwar project-state's accomplishments— key among them taming capital and building the welfare state—was "an alternative state project in its own right." On this score, he echoes Quinn Slobodian's argument in *Globalists* (2018), suggesting another weakness of the *Economist*'s flat talk of "the state" having returned—a claim that assumes it had actually disappeared. In reality, neoliberals didn't abandon state power; they redirected it for their own ends.

BEFORE STATES can take on projects they must first exist. But when, exactly, is a state born? The successors to the Austro-Hungarian Empire have often been held up as an easy case. According to a familiar story, these states sprung fully formed from the minds of nationalist statesmen immediately after the demise of the Habsburg monarchy. Wheatley shows that real story of the birth, life, and death of states in Central Europe is much more complex.

One reason the true history is messier than often supposed, she demonstrates, is that many of the central political actors in the era claimed that these states *couldn't* be born at this moment—because they were already alive. Austria-Hungary was an "intricately layered, prodigiously complex empire," she stresses, one that had accrued its territories over many centuries by absorbing many formerly distinct legal entities. As the empire crumbled in 1918, politicians and others aspiring for national autonomy or independence in Bohemia, Moravia, Silesia, and elsewhere argued that these old legal jurisdictions—"their original legal standing, their original independence"—"had survived long centuries of imperial rule intact." Their ancient polities, they claimed, had been "swallowed up but not dissolved in the python of empire." As Georg Jellinek, a Viennese jurist at the center of Wheatley's study, argued in 1900, the territorial expansion of the empire "was not accompanied by an explicit declaration of the de-state-ification of its parts." "The moment at which the Bohemian lands entirely lost their state character cannot be determined with complete certainty," he maintained.

Czechs and Hungarians especially relied on this theory of statehood when pressing for independence after World War I. As the Hungarian delegation to the Paris Peace Conference claimed,

> Hungary is no new State born of the dismemberment of the Austro-Hungarian Monarchy. . . . As far as public law the Hungary of to-day is the same State she has been through her past of a thousand years. She kept her position as an independent State on entering a union with Austria and during the whole existence of this union.

This view had several advantages for advocates. It not only spared them the trouble of establishing "new" states; Wheatley demonstrates that it also allowed nationalist activists to claim the legality and legitimacy of the Habsburg empire itself—since the leaders were respecting the imperial legal framework that had tenderly preserved their beloved frozen kingdoms for so long.

The most difficult questions, Wheatley shows, pertained to the birth of Austria. With the Settlement of 1867, the empire was divided in two halves, each fully and equally sovereign. The eastern half was easily identifiable: the Kingdom of Hungary. The western half had a more ambiguous identity: it was known formally as the Kingdoms and Lands Represented in the Imperial Parliament, less formally as Cisleithania (because it was on "this side" of the Leitha River; Hungary being on the other), and informally (but incorrectly) as Austria. When the empire fell apart, it was not clear what was to be done with this territorial rump. "German Austria," observed Austromarxist intellectual and politician Otto Bauer in 1923, "is nothing but the reminder that was left over from the old empire when the other nations fell away from it." (Visitors to grand, gilded Vienna may still feel this way while strolling the Ringstrasse.) In the end, it was the Allied powers that christened the territory the "Republic of Austria."

Naming the country was the least of the worries, however. The real issues concerned legal continuity: Which country was the legal successor to the Habsburg Empire? The leaders of the new Austrian Republic were emphatic that it wasn't them. "The Danube Monarchy," the Austrian chancellor explained to the Paris Peace Conference in 1919, "ceased to exist on 12 November, 1918." Everything that happened before, Austrian diplomats argued, "has no more upon German-Austria than on Czecho-Slovakia or any other national State which has arisen on Austrian-Hungarian soil."

In all these cases, abstract questions of theory became very concrete. "Political events of the present," as one Austrian jurist put it in 1919, "present various problems of legal science that, until now, were only objects of theoretical investigation." These "political events," moreover, created legal problems of grave concern to ordinary citizens, not just politicians and lawyers. The end of the Habsburg Empire and formation of new nation-states left many thousands of people legally stateless citizens of nowhere.

In her recent book *Statelessness* (2020), historian Mira Siegelberg traces how formerly Austro-Hungarian and Russian thinkers approached the problem of statelessness after World War I in ways that opened new democratic and cosmopolitan possibilities, including designs for robust international organizations and visions of just world orders. (This was before the even greater crisis of statelessness after World War II contributed to the foreclosure of these possibilities and helped solidify the hegemony of the nation-state as "the sole legitimate organizing unit of global politics," as Siegelberg puts it.) But on the ground, those whose imperial passports were abruptly made meaningless experienced the life-upending consequences of state death.

WITH WARS RAGING in Gaza and Ukraine, concrete questions of state birth and state death are back in the news. A longer-term worry stems from rising sea levels, extreme weather events, and many other consequences of a warming planet. What will happen to the states of

Nauru and Kiribati if their territories sink beneath the waves? How will states cope with climate-induced migration? More proactively, can states cooperate to drive global carbon emissions to zero? The problems that climate change poses for statehood may be exceeded only by the problems that statehood poses for the possibility of a habitable planet.

This fact is reflected very differently in these three books. Pettit, for his part, mentions climate change just twice. He first identifies it as one of a small number of catastrophes that could cause the state to be "disrupted or undone" as a political form, and then he suggests that future human flourishing rests on "how states perform" when faced with "climate change, pandemic threat, chronic deprivation, and the eruptions of inhumanity that seem to come with our genes." Hard to disagree there.

Maier says more. On the one hand, he identifies climate change as a major cause of the contemporary world's "sense of untethering," and he notes that the project-state itself was a major cause of skyrocketing greenhouse gases during the postwar "Great Acceleration" of carbon-fueled growth. On the other hand, his narrative suggests that a strong state—with a "transformative agenda"—offers a potential solution.

It might seem that Maier is headed to an embrace of the Green New Deal state. In fact, he comes to a different conclusion: "Perhaps the individual project-state should no longer suffice as an aspiration but given the scale of the global challenges must ultimately form part of an international society." Given the book's focus on global networks of capital and governance, it is may not be surprising that Maier finds the state both limited and limiting. The scale of governance must match the scale of the problems, he suggests. But though he approvingly gestures to mid-twentieth-century visions for new models of statehood and international order, he doesn't mention that in every single case they failed.

A major factor in each failure was the allure of sovereignty, which still stands in the way of international "projects" today. Take the UN Framework Convention on Climate Change (UNFCCC), the 1992 treaty that established the international architecture for tackling global warming. Its signatories echo Maier's argument, acknowledging that a changing climate is "a common concern of humankind" and that "the global nature of climate change calls for the widest possible cooperation by all countries . . . and appropriate international response." But then the treaty snaps back to form, explicitly reaffirming "the principle of sovereignty of States" and "the sovereign right [of states] to exploit their own resources." If we hope for "international society" to come to the rescue, we are going to need a new approach to sovereignty.

This observation isn't new; sovereignty has long been the bugbear of those who hope for greater global cooperation. Already in 1934, legal philosopher Hans Kelsen—a student-turned-rival of Jellinek, and also one of Wheatley's central characters—condemned "the ossifying absolutism of the dogma of sovereignty." In its place, he sought to develop a new theory that "relativizes the state" and places it in a "continuous sequence of legal structures, gradually merging into one another."

This is a radically different vision than the dogma enshrined in international law and politics today, which rests on "the singularity of sovereignty," as Wheatley observes: "the notion of a single, supreme, undivided power." Habsburg thinkers didn't recognize their world in this model, developed by English and French thinkers. Instead they sought a sovereignty that rang true to their "layer cake" of a polity—a state structure that Pettit, without citing its most important contemporary theorist Elinor Ostrom, calls "polycentric." Theorizing from the center of Europe, these thinkers found that sovereignty came in many hues and gradations; it wasn't black and white. Wheatley's recovery of their work makes clear that "neither 'state' nor 'sovereignty' can be taken as fixed, pregiven things." New concepts and theories in hand, Habsburg theorists imagined new forms of national and international order.

The unmooring of absolutist concepts of the state and sovereignty could be useful for new governance projects at the scale of the challenges we face. Deploying Habsburgian tools, rather than Anglo-French ones, we might imagine a planetary project-state that avoids becoming the "climate leviathan" that Joel Wainwright and Geoff Mann have depicted—a "coherent planetary sovereign" that absorbs, countermands, or otherwise annihilates the sovereignty of all existing states. Wheatley notes that as Jellinek saw it, "the defining characteristic of a sovereign state was that it could be bound only by itself. . . . Precisely because a sovereign state had unlimited final authority over itself, it could decide to bind itself to another and give up some of its rights." On this view, it is confidence in the strength and legitimacy of your own sovereignty that permits modifications to it.

Wheatley gives a striking example of such sovereign self-assurance. In 1904, Hungarian statesman Count Albert Apponyi

Blake

gave a lecture attacking the "widespread fundamental error" that considers the "Austrian empire . . . the primordial fact, and whatever is known of Hungarian independence as a sort of provincial autonomy." He explained:

> The primordial fact is an independent kingdom of Hungary, which has allied itself for certain purposes and under certain conditions to the equally independent and distinct empire of Austria, by an act of sovereign free will, without having ever abdicated the smallest particle of its sovereignty as an independent nation, though it has consented to exercise a small part of its governmental functions through executive organs common with Austria.

Arguments of this sort illustrate how international cooperation need not be perceived as coming at the expense of national sovereignty. And indeed, this attitude is evident in the rhetoric of actually existing international cooperation—including the UNFCCC and the UN Charter itself.

There is a flip side to this reasoning, of course. Ceding one's sovereignty is difficult when it is *not* felt to be secure. This fact helps to explain why, of all the multinational federated political structures proposed or tried in the decades after World War II, the only one to survive was the European Economic Community and its successors. The wealthy and well-established states of Europe, not the poor and inchoate states of the postcolonial world, were willing to voluntarily abrogate their own sovereignty in order to facilitate "common action" toward "economic and social progress," in the words of the 1957 Treaty of Rome.

In a world still marked by grave power imbalances, overcoming these obstacles will not be easy. But we should not consider it impossible. Efforts to shift the balance of global power away from the U.S.-led "liberal international order" are afoot, from China's Belt and Road Initiative to the recent expansion of the BRICS+ bloc. And renewed interest in the Group of 77's 1974 proposal for a "New International Economic Order," a largely forgotten episode in the global struggle for justice, may offer a "usable past" from which new political projects can be launched.

There is much creative thinking to be done. Like the Habsburg jurists who watched their imperial home collapse, we—all citizens of an overheating, interconnected planet—are at a critical juncture. Wheatley draws on political theorist Adom Getachew's work on "worldmaking after empire" in the Black Atlantic to argue that "the bracing experience of new statehood made questions of international order existential and drove new theories and projects at the scale of the world." The challenge of climate change demands similar thinking today. Whether the state is a part of our collective future—or whether it gives way to alternative forms of sovereignty and instruments of rule—is, as Maier puts it, "up for grabs."

Blake

PRISON REFORM'S SHELL GAME

Bonnie Tenneriello

I FIRST SAW Davongie Stone last year through a small window in a very solid cell door. Representing Prisoners' Legal Services, where I work as an attorney, I was touring a unit in Massachusetts's maximum-security prison as a member of an oversight committee created by a 2018 criminal justice reform law. After years of grassroots pressure, the state legislature had passed measures intended to limit the use of solitary confinement, a practice that the United Nations Special Rapporteur has said can amount to torture.

We were there to observe the transformation of what had previously been called the Restrictive Housing Unit (RHU), one of the many euphemisms Massachusetts has employed for solitary confinement. The unit was now known as a Behavioral Assessment Unit (BAU), part of a revamp that officials like to say has ended solitary in the state's prison system. An even older defunct name for solitary—Special Management Unit—was still stenciled on the doors.

Stone is a tall, young Black man with long dreadlocks and a serious demeanor. He recalls being sent to the unit because he had refused to live with a cellmate. Suffering from severe PTSD, bipolar disorder, and anxiety, he was overwhelmed by the idea of being locked in a cell with someone else nearly all day. He had come into the system six years before we met, at twenty years old, with all the things that funnel people into incarceration—childhood abuse, entry into foster care and then the juvenile justice system, and brown skin. When he was twelve, a psychological evaluator described him as "a young man who has experienced a debilitating degree of trauma and uncertainty in his environment" and noted among his strengths, "he is intelligent, is genuinely interested in others, and strives to remain hopeful about his future." He landed in prison for a violent offense at twenty-one.

Stone has spent most of his prison time locked in a cell in various secure units, but the system has not spent time helping him. He has not gotten the help he seeks for managing his trauma and anger, nor has he had access to rehabilitative programs to prepare him for his chance at parole or his release at the end of his sentence in two years. When he presented video testimony to the state legislature earlier this year on a far more comprehensive reform bill, he said that the supermax prison "only breeds despair, anger, and hatred. It is not conducive to rehabilitation."

Incarcerated people and their allies have struggled for many years against solitary confinement, the harms of which are now broadly acknowledged by medical and mental health experts and professional organizations. We have seen important victories in New York, New

Jersey, Colorado, and Ohio, as well as in Massachusetts. All these states have ended or at least curtailed the worst abuses.

Yet correctional systems have an uncanny ability to neutralize reform. The standard definition of "solitary confinement" is being locked in a cell for twenty-two hours or more a day. Prisons have realized that by increasing time out of cell by just an hour a day, they can define solitary away—no matter if prisoners still have extremely restricted freedom of movement in that little bit of extra time. This is exactly what has happened in Massachusetts, and the state is not alone: an array of similar arrangements have cropped up following solitary reforms in other places, all relying on forms of containment that either resemble solitary or come very close. Prisons never seem to run out of people deemed too dangerous to leave their cells unless they are isolated or physically restrained.

What's more, Massachusetts's disproportionately Black and brown prison population still lives at the mercy of a largely white correctional staff, who are both afraid of those they oversee and able to exercise largely unchecked discretion over who gets punished and for what. The state incarcerates half the number of people it did ten years ago, but the budget of the Department of Corrections (DOC) is higher than it was then, even after adjusting for inflation—in part because the system employs an unusually high number of correctional officers. Can meaningful solitary reform be achieved in a system where surveillance and control are the lodestar and deprivation is pervasive?

For their part, DOC administrators express pride in the new system, and its architects—consultants with Falcon Correctional and

Community Services—report receiving a flood of inquiries from other jurisdictions impressed by the Massachusetts changes. The model thus looks set to metastasize further still.

Incarcerated people and their advocates are desperately hoping for better. Among other things, the bill that Stone spoke on behalf of—still scheduled to be voted on in committee—calls for at least eight hours out of cell for all incarcerated people, community standards of medical, mental health, and substance abuse care, and universal access to rehabilitative programs and education throughout the prison system. Stone raised a key question in his testimony. "Why is it that DOC gets so much money but continues to take everything away from us?" he asked. "Where is this money going?"

THE 2018 reform law, known as the Criminal Justice Reform Act, included provisions designed to limit the use of solitary confinement, which the law calls "restrictive housing." In broad strokes, it states that people can only be held in such housing for two reasons: as a disciplinary sanction, or as a temporary measure while they are deemed to pose an "unacceptable risk" to prison safety. It specifies that everyone in the latter group must be given periodic reviews to determine whether they continue to pose such a risk; it mandates minimum conditions and privileges; and it bans the use of such housing for certain people, including those with serious mental illness and those held for their own protection—unless administrators certify that there is no other appropriate place for them and efforts are being made to find one.

Tenneriello

The DOC complied with the law and looked further, hiring Falcon to do a system-wide assessment. A six-person team—including former heads of the Colorado and Connecticut prison systems and other leading correctional reformers—submitted a report in March 2021. Among other things, it recommended dissolving the state's notorious Department Disciplinary Unit, where men had been held in solitary for up to ten years; considering the elimination of all restrictive housing as it was "currently defined"; and tailoring specialized units to an individual's particular "criminogenic needs," building upon a Secure Adjustment Unit that the DOC had opened to divert people excluded from restrictive housing by the 2018 law.

The DOC publicly embraced the report, promising to implement its recommendations and even end restrictive housing in all its forms. By 2023, the Department Disciplinary Unit was closed in a widely applauded and long overdue move, and RHUs had been rebranded as BAUs. According to the DOC's description, people are assigned to these units if they are deemed to pose a safety risk. They are supposed to have their needs "expeditiously" assessed while in the unit, and the DOC says they are allowed at least three hours out of cell daily, as well as a weekly, one-hour group "wellness program."

People held in BAUs see it differently. Those I have spoken with still call it "the hole" and say it doesn't feel much different than before. Time "out of cell" is spent either in an outdoor cage like a dog run or indoors with one ankle and one arm shackled to a table or chair, which feels more restraining than a cell to many. Their commissary purchases are significantly restricted. They must eat meals alone in their cells, and their contact with the outside world is severely limited; while prisoners in the general population have unlimited access to calls and, even in maximum security, three visits a week, those in BAUs are allowed only four twenty-minute phone calls and at most two one-hour visits behind glass each week. And the DOC says that the extra hour out of cell means that these units technically no longer count as "restrictive housing," so the protections of the 2018 reform law—including required reviews, minimum conditions, and the exclusion of vulnerable individuals—do not apply.

In response to concerns that my office and others have raised about these conditions, the DOC has stated that the stays are short-term. (In reality, according to legal filings from the DOC itself, people have been held in the unit for weeks or even many months.) Moreover, an administrator told me, offering full commissary purchases might lead people to resist being transferred out, since they would lose what they had purchased. (Why they couldn't just keep what they purchased is unclear.) As for the limited out-of-cell time and the use of restraints, the DOC says that allowing people who might be enemies to mix unshackled in a BAU would be unsafe, and figuring out which individuals could mingle without restraints requires too much staff and space. (Yet some people held in BAUs are accused only of nonviolent offenses.)

After detention in a BAU, people are either sent back to regular housing units or classified to one of the new Secure Adjustment Units (SAUs), where they are supposed to receive programming according to their assessed needs. SAUs range from the punitive but less restrictive units in medium security to the most restrictive, known as SAU IV, located in the maximum-security Souza-Baranowski Correctional Center.

SAU IV allows the same three hours daily of so-called recreation as the BAU, though conditions are slightly eased in the later stages of the SAU program. As in the BAU, isolation is compounded by limited visits, always behind glass, and scarce phone calls. Many commissary items are not available at all in SAUs, while other items are on an "incentive list," meaning that they are allowed only for good behavior. Any of these meager allotments can be taken away for a disciplinary violation, leaving people locked in cells totally deprived of contact with loved ones outside.

The stakes are highest in SAU IV because it is a housing assignment, not a "temporary" placement like the BAUs. People can be held there for between eighteen months and six years at the discretion of correctional staff. Frustration over the extreme deprivations in the unit, along with a climate of violence and unaccountability, have led to turmoil and allegations of abuse. And as in BAUs, the DOC maintains that three hours a day outside the sleeping cell (even if in shackles and cages) exempts SAU IV from the 2018 protections. This leads to a bitter irony: SAU IV is in many ways *more* restrictive than the prison's former RHUs. And this fact has only fueled anger and resistance, met in turn with violent retaliation from corrections officers.

DOMINIC REZENDES came to SAU IV in January 2020, straight from solitary in the DDU. Of Cape Verdean descent, with a mustache and beard, facial tattoos, and braided hair, the thirty-three year old has been in the DOC since twenty-two, after a childhood entangled with the child welfare and juvenile justice systems. "My whole life has been institutions," he told me earlier this year. "It was just easier to put me away." He thinks he has been in isolation for about three-quarters of his eleven years in prison.

Rezendes was one of nineteen people in SAU IV who launched a hunger strike on October 6 last year to protest conditions in the unit. They reached out to the attorney general's office to seek an investigation, noting in a statement that the unit "has mirrored the same conditions as those previous restrictive housing units." In fact, protests had been going on for some time. In June, people held there filed grievances and demanded to speak with leadership. On June 14, after conflict over their TVs being taken away (a vital diversion in the unit), twenty-six people in the unit were reportedly violently attacked by corrections officers in the guise of "cell extractions." (Also known as "forced moves," these involve a team of officers in riot gear entering a prisoner's cell; they are the most common form of guard assaults.) In late August, eleven more were reportedly assaulted in the guise of cell extractions.

In early January this year, a man in the unit started a fire in his cell in frustration over lack of medical attention to an injured hand. Allegations of abuse have continued to surface—people being locked in the outdoor cages for hours, medical neglect for a gastrointestinal disease that caused vomiting and diarrhea, and feces left in uncleaned cells. Reports of assaults continued into the new year, and some of the most vocal protesters were moved to more restrictive BAUs in other facilities.

Then, in early February, Rezendes also started a fire in his cell; he told me he did so after repeatedly telling guards he was having a mental health crisis but getting no response. A little over a week before, he had testified to the state legislature alongside Stone. With less than a year left before his release, he told lawmakers, he could not access any help with reentry. "There has been minimal opportunity for me to progress myself in any way, shape, or form," he said. Having lost his mother, father, child, and brother, he noted he had "nobody to go back home to. . . . I have no trajectory, and there's no one here to help me." When I spoke with him the day after the fire, while he was under mental health observation, he told me he had wanted to die. "I have never done anything like that in my life. I was just hopeless. I thought if I create a big enough issue, maybe nobody else would have to feel the way I felt."

People held in SAU IV are entitled to take a rehabilitative class, but many don't participate. They must be shackled to do so, and unlike prisoners in general population, they do not get "good time"—sentence reduction credits—for their work. In principle, they can get good time for other programs, but such courses have long waiting lists, and even if they get in, they only have access to the ones that can be done alone in your cell. That rules most courses out. This is yet another way that the new unit is worse than old solitary. The 2018 reform law required that good time programs be offered in RHUs, but the DOC maintains this provision does not apply to BAUs and SAUs.

SAU IV's deprivations and allegations of abuse are not exceptional in the maximum-security prison that houses it. Much of its general population of more than 900 people lives in conditions close to restrictive housing; more than half—those held in the "Northside" units—are allowed personal visits only through glass partitions. As one Northside resident told my office, "We get no sunlight, no yard, no gym, no school, no programs, and just no movement [outside of their units] at all. . . . I have PTSD that is getting worse and I'm developing schizophrenic symptoms from being over here." In January 2020, following attacks on guards that took place in one unit, correction officers carried out a prison-wide rampage; more than 100 incarcerated people reported assaults.

THE DOC's reliance on harsh security measures in all these settings reflects the system's overall priorities. On average, the DOC spent $138,500 per person in custody last year, much of it on security rather than prisoner welfare. The state now has one correctional officer for just over every two people in prison, and officers make up half the DOC labor force. As of 2019—the most recent year comparisons were available—Massachusetts had the fourth highest correctional officer-to-prisoner ratio of any state in the nation. And the state's correctional officers raked in $45 million in overtime last year, with indications that substantial amounts were improperly approved and falsified.

With such high staffing, each incarcerated person lives under constant surveillance by correctional staff and constant threat of discipline

Tenneriello

if they break one of the myriad, arbitrarily enforced rules. Meanwhile, those looking for growth, education, or treatment go frustrated. In its report, Falcon stresses the importance of assessing criminogenic thought and behavior among prisoners who commit disciplinary violations, but meaningful change requires addressing the criminogenic nature of the prison system itself, which routinely deprives people in custody of minimally humane treatment and meaningful activity and leaves correctional staff largely unaccountable for abuses large and small.

The most recent available data shows that in December 2022, only one in five people in custody in Massachusetts were in any kind of rehabilitative, mental health, substance use, educational, or vocational program or on a work assignment. By the last available count, the DOC was spending only some 4 percent of its budget on programs. Data obtained by my office through a 2023 public record request shows that in six medium- and maximum-security DOC facilities alone, over 1,500 people were on a waiting list for the DOC's substance use program. Another 107 people were waiting for the sex offender treatment program, 427 for the reentry readiness workshop, 533 for a course called "Criminal Thinking—Thinking for a Change," and 507 for "Emotional Awareness."

Medical and mental health care in Massachusetts prisons, as in nearly all others, is privatized and grossly inadequate. Across the country, an estimated 44 percent of people in jail and 37 percent in prison have a mental illness, in contrast to around 20 percent of the general population. Yet while psychiatric medications are commonly prescribed in the DOC, those in need of mental health counseling typically see a clinician just once a month.

The situation is similar when it comes to substance use disorders, though here the need is generally even higher. About 63 percent of people in jail and 58 percent in prison suffer from one, yet access to appropriate treatment remains scarce. Medication-assisted treatment has improved greatly in Massachusetts, thanks to legislative action, but in most cases those who were not prescribed a medication for opioid use disorder in the community struggle to access it in prisons and jails. In too many instances, even people who are prescribed treatments for opioid addiction before incarceration must taper off while in prison, only to resume before release. Those serving life sentences may never have access to medically assisted treatment. Meanwhile, rates of illegal drug use are high throughout the system.

Underinvestment in opportunities and treatment leaves control and punishment as the primary means of keeping order. People with histories of trauma and unmanaged mental health issues get into conflicts, and people without access to substance treatment have easy access to contraband drugs; in too many cases, the system puts such people in restrictive forms of confinement rather than offering necessary support.

These warped priorities also contribute to overincarceration. Lack of access to programs denies people "good time" and reduces their chances for parole; along with scarce treatment, it also leaves people unprepared to succeed on release. A recently released DOC study found that people who received substance abuse treatment or education while in prison had markedly lower recidivism rates after one year than a cohort whose needs were not met. The broad failure to

Tenneriello

meet these needs carries a human cost far greater than the average of $138,500 a year the state now spends on those it reincarcerates—and the costs are not borne equally.

There is no data on the racial composition of the SAUs and BAUs, but there are good reasons to believe that Black and Hispanic incarcerated people are punished disproportionately. A largely white correctional staff supervises a population where Black and brown people are extremely overrepresented due to inequity at every stage of the criminal legal system. According to Bureau of Justice Statistics data, Black, non-Hispanic people make up 7 percent of the Massachusetts population but 29 percent of those in state prisons, while Hispanic people account for 12 percent of the population but 25 percent of state prisoners. These disparities have only grown as the Massachusetts prison and jail population has declined, since the white prison population has seen the highest rate of decrease.

At the same time, particularly in state prisons, the staff is drawn from largely white surrounding rural areas, attracted to well-paid prison jobs. Corrections officers write disciplinary reports at their own discretion, and guilt is generally adjudicated by a fellow correctional officer, leaving every person in custody fearful of incurring a grudge or even displeasure. Thus, punishment is racialized. And disciplinary convictions lead to punitive housing assignments, higher security classifications, diminished parole and earned good time opportunities, and therefore longer time in prison or jail and higher prison and jail populations. Earlier this year I asked a resident of SAU IV what the racial breakdown was; he estimated that of the twenty-six people held in the two phases of the program, perhaps two or three were not Black or brown.

Along with a racialized system of punishment comes racialized violence. Last year my organization received forty-two reports of assaults on thirty-two people held in SAU IV, some attacks on the same person; at least thirteen of those reportedly assaulted were Black, and all of those reporting multiple assaults were Black or Hispanic.

In addition to the comprehensive reform Stone and Rezendes spoke in support of earlier this year, the Massachusetts legislature is currently considering creating an office to "facilitate the recommendations of the Special Legislative Commission on Structural Racism in Correctional Facilities of the Commonwealth." If passed, this first-of-its-kind legislation would establish an independent oversight body responsible for the investigation and elimination of structural and systemic racism in the state's carceral system and data on racial disparities that is now lacking. But in a system that gives unfettered discretion to largely white staff and administrators overseeing a disproportionately Black and brown prison population, it is reasonable to expect disparities in all of these areas.

MASSACHUSETTS HAS closed three minimum- and medium-security prisons in recent years, significantly reducing overhead, and another large medium-security prison is slated to close. Meanwhile, the state's plan to replace its deteriorating women's prison with a newer, bigger one—despite the small, aging female population—has drawn fire. A moratorium on prison construction passed both chambers of the state legislature during the tenure of former governor Charlie Baker, who vetoed it, but if passed again, current governor Maura Healey might sign it.

Reducing the footprint of incarceration as populations dwindle clearly makes sense, but it is difficult to say whether this will be reflected in better conditions for those remaining in custody. Correctional budgets are opaque, and corrections departments maintain that population reduction doesn't translate simply into savings, as facility maintenance and other fixed costs don't drop proportionately and costs such as health care continue to grow. As MassINC notes in a recent report, it is hard to know how much the DOC is saving and how those savings are being used.

One hard-to-move factor is correctional staffing. Massachusetts's extremely high ratio of guards to prisoners is unlikely to decline any time soon, not least since DOC corrections officers have a strong and powerful union. When prisons are closed, officers assigned there are being redeployed to other prisons rather than laid off. In turn, the strength of the union makes it harder to pass reform—whether because reallocating funds to rehabilitative programming and away from security might entail layoffs, or because correctional officers resist any perceived threat to their power and safety. The argument the union makes publicly is that reforms have bred violence; indeed, the union blamed the events of January 2020 on the 2018 reform law, even though no studies have shown that solitary confinement makes prisons safer.

The stress and danger of prison is real, of course, but there is no symmetry between the experience of corrections officers and the people they guard. Rezendes expresses both understanding of the pressure officers face and helplessness at being at their mercy. For the officers, he has told me, "this is not a job, it's a culture. If they do what's right, they get ostracized. They either quit or they do what [other corrections officers] want them to do. They go home, but for us we get [criminal] cases, we get beatings."

Change will require acknowledging that prison violence, so often cited to justify draconian practices, is also a product of those practices. And it will require recognizing that even in lower-security settings, lives are being wasted and endangered by a system that funds control rather than human development.

In recent years, some states have taken important steps to reduce incarceration. In addition to solitary reform, Massachusetts's 2018 reform law included a number of measures of this sort—from bail reform and new pathways for diversion to the elimination of some mandatory minimum sentences and certain court-imposed fees and fines that can land people back in prison for nonpayment. These measures may not be responsible for the entire drop in both incarceration and violent crime that the state has experienced since then, and they are far from sufficient, but they reflect growing awareness that incarceration can make communities less safe.

The case for change inside prisons resonates with this shift away from incarceration. Just as communities deprived of housing, decent jobs, and decent schools have been ravaged by mass incarceration, so are the incarcerated sons and daughters of those communities deprived of care, opportunity, and dignity in prison. And when we can't control them, we cage them in a prison within a prison—call it what you will.

FOR A SOLIDARITY STATE
Leah Hunt-Hendrix & Astra Taylor

ON A SUMMER afternoon in 1966, an estimated six thousand welfare recipients rallied around the United States in twenty-five cities. Children in tow, the women held forth in public squares, marched on state capitols, and occupied local welfare offices as part of the first cross-country demonstration of recipients of Aid to Families with Dependent Children. They demanded better benefits and—in the words of the two thousand–strong New York City contingent—an end to what they called the "indignities" of the welfare system, which they viewed as a patriarchal and punitive government bureaucracy. In place of meager checks, invasive surveillance, and constant shaming, they called for a guaranteed annual income and insisted that people impacted by policy should have a say in its implementation.

Most of the women were Black, but a good number of white women signed on as well. Their actions launched a powerful national movement—the National Welfare Rights Organization (NWRO)—that aimed to increase material support for all struggling families and create the foundation of a care-based economy. Its militancy and rapid growth opened an opportunity to alter the relationship of the state to its citizens, and the movement brought concrete reforms—though the movement would be undone by the changing political climate of the mid-1970s, when the War on Poverty gave way to the War on Crime.

Ever since, progressives have been fighting to salvage remnants of the liberal welfare state. They are right to push for more egalitarian policies, whether in the form of higher taxation, more generous public provision, or a stronger regulatory regime. But as the NWRO made clear, the social and emotional dimensions of statecraft are just as key. As we forge a more equitable social contract, we also need to change the character of our social relationships and arrangements. A new approach—rooted in the ethic of solidarity—should be our north star.

State policies play a huge role in determining social conditions, from the amount of carbon in the atmosphere to the cost of rent. They also shape our perceptions of the world, each other, and even ourselves. Conservatives have long understood this and sought to wield state power to remake citizens in their ideal mold. "Economics are the method," the former British Prime Minister Margaret Thatcher said in 1981. "The object is to change the soul." Because the state structures the society and systems in which we live, it can make us more prone to care for one another and collaborate constructively—or more inclined to compete for seemingly scarce resources, more mistrustful and afraid. These feedback loops are powerful forces that can tear society apart or help weave it back together.

In recent decades, and in no small part due to the influence of Thatcher and her neoliberal allies, social programs in the United States have been structured in ways that stymie and suppress solidarity, obscuring the fact of our fundamental interdependence by promoting individualism and competition instead of cooperation and reciprocity. Part of the problem is what Suzanne Mettler calls the "submerged state." While aid to the poor is stingy and highly stigmatized, as the NWRO organizers knew firsthand, government benefits to the middle class and affluent are generous and mostly go unnoticed. They inspire neither shame nor appreciation in part because they are structured to be delivered through more passive mechanisms, such as tax breaks and subsidies. The mortgage interest deduction, for example, rewards those who are wealthy enough to buy a home.

In place of these mechanisms, we should structure policies and programs in ways that reveal the formative role the state plays in everyone's life while also bringing our interdependence to the fore. In a word, we need a *solidarity state*.

HOW CAN WE get there? The American Climate Corps (ACC), created through an executive order in 2023, is a modest step in the right direction. Like the Works Progress Administration of the New Deal era, programs that provide dignified and well-paid jobs and create obvious public benefits are a clear way for government to play a positive role in many people's lives. The ACC promised to provide

Hunt-Hendrix & Taylor

twenty thousand jobs, but by October last year—just one month after the program's announcement—it had already drawn forty-two thousand sign-ups. There is clear demand for these opportunities, and the more abundant and accessible they are, the more they will be seen as evidence of the government's potentially constructive role in ordinary people's lives.

Imagine if every individual were encouraged and incentivized to participate in such a program as a duty of citizenship. Within the Solidarity State framework, such programs would offer opportunities to perform public service that leaves people and the planet better off, imparting skills and experience while also leaving participants more connected to and invested in the common good. As things stand, the U.S. government routinely prioritizes what historian Micol Seigel calls "violence work." Police, prison guards, immigration officers, and soldiers are generously subsidized by the state—teachers, therapists, conservationists, far less so. We see care work as an essential way to build communal, solidaristic social bonds.

In the nineteenth century, the industrial revolution upended and remade social relations. During that period, the political tendency known as solidarism argued that the state's primary function should be to create social cohesion among its citizens. In large part, this meant protecting people from the abuses of power that come with consolidated wealth. The solidarists were radical republicans—they emphasized citizens' participation in self-governance, envisioning worker cooperatives as preferable to the burgeoning corporate sector, and credit unions as the future of finance. These were upper-class thinkers—indeed, one of their leaders was even named Léon Bourgeois—who often downplayed the role of class conflict and exploitation. Nevertheless, their thinking offers a series of useful prompts to imagining a political alternative to the status quo.

Liberal political philosophy—the intellectual tradition that formed that basis of the liberal welfare state—draws on social contract theory, which argues that society was forged by a contract between rational, autonomous men in a state of nature. The solidarists rejected the premise of this abstraction. Instead, they argued that from the moment we are born, we are already enmeshed in quasi-contracts: we inherit a world made by those who came before us, and we are indebted to the future generations to whom we will leave the world when we pass on. No one is ever fully independent or self-made. Rather, we are all born owing what they dubbed "social debts"—not the debts that are imposed on individuals by predatory creditors, but the debts that tie us together and hold us as both givers and receivers, beneficiaries and benefactors, in a shared society. They also spoke of social property as opposed to private property, recognizing that all property gains its value from its social context and should, in turn, offer benefits more broadly; they emphasized duties and obligations as much as individual rights. They also emphasized the need for restorative justice, aware that past harms must be repaired if we hope to forge solidarity and create a more peaceful and prosperous society.

Updating some of their ideas for our time, we suggest that a solidarity state would be based on four key principles: participation, parity, pluralism, and peace.

First, we see the opportunity to participate in creating one's society—beyond the ballot box—as critical. The welfare state often

Hunt-Hendrix & Taylor

treats its citizens as recipients of charity, with the state as a provider of services bequeathed from on high. A solidarity state would instead treat us as active and empowered agents of change. The history of the Community Action Programs, the centerpiece of LBJ's War on Poverty, offers a short-lived but instructive example. These programs empowered individuals to work together to address local issues, essentially providing government funding for local organizing, some of which was impressively effective and even militant. Under its auspices tenants organized rent strikes and rankled local officials. Head Start, Volunteers in Service to America, summer youth programs, and meal programs all came out of this moment. But under Nixon, and then Reagan, funding was cut and these programs were whittled down to bare bones.

Second, parity is necessary to a solidarity state. In contrast to the liberal welfare state at its heyday, a solidarity state would operate on the premise that you cannot successfully wage a war on poverty without simultaneously waging a war on concentrated wealth and the concentrated power that wealth can purchase. And you certainly cannot win it by treating the poor themselves as the enemy, as the War on Crime effectively did.

In addition to policies that support redistribution, a solidarity state would achieve parity by promoting predistribution—in other words, by closing the wealth gap well before taxes are levied. This process would go beyond improving or expanding the services the state provides. Instead, it would democratize control over how society's resources—including the state itself—are owned, distributed, and run. For example, a reparative approach to finance might invest in communities and households that have long been victims of predatory lending or denied access to credit; it could create green social housing in neighborhoods devastated by redlining or open public banks currently exploited by payday lenders and check-cashing companies. It could build on the legislation that Rhode Island passed in 2022 to legalize cannabis, which sets aside a substantial portion of limited retail licenses for worker-owned businesses. This is the largest expansion of state support for cooperative enterprises in recent history and a way of explicitly ensuring that income and opportunities will flow to the low-income communities most harmed by the War on Drugs.

Third, we do not see pluralism as a hindrance to social cohesion but as something that should be fostered. Pluralism need not be divisive if given a context where differences can be acknowledged and embraced. Today liberals and conservatives often insist that homogeneity is a prerequisite for a stable welfare state. Take political scientist Yascha Mounk's recent book *The Great Experiment* (2022), which argues that liberal countries are in crisis, and welfare states are in decline, largely because they are diverse in terms of political perspectives, religious convictions, racial and ethnic identities, and gender and sexual orientations. But the data on whether heterogeneity always leads to social conflict is mixed at best.

In contrast, we believe that plutocracy, not pluralism, is the problem. Anti-immigrant sentiment is often driven by elites who want to deflect responsibility for low wages and inadequate safety nets. In our view, solidarity must be consciously cultivated—its presence or absence is not preordained. This means demography is not destiny, but rather an opportunity to connect people across their differences. Consider one

Hunt-Hendrix & Taylor

interesting example from Canada, where the state provides small groups of private citizens the opportunity to sponsor refugees. Sponsors are expected to help get them set up with housing, schools, and doctors, and supply food, clothing, and other forms of material and emotional assistance. They are even encouraged to "introduce newcomers to people with similar personal interests" according to the Canadian government's website, a statement which is attuned to the crucial role social ties play in individual and collective wellbeing.

This program inverts the logic that sees citizens as consumers of benefits, fighting each other for scraps. Instead, it fosters solidarity: citizens work with the government to provide for people who have fled their home regions in search of safety or opportunity. In this way, the program offers more democratic and dignified roles for all parties. We must develop ways to cultivate solidarity by enabling diverse people and groups to collaborate and coexist on scales small and large, whether through refugee assistance programs, truly integrated schools and neighborhoods, citizens' assemblies, multicultural or plurinational governance structures, or any range of other pluralistic and participation-enhancing public initiatives.

Finally, we need to make peace a central pillar of our society. As Coretta Scott King said in 1975, "this nation has never honestly dealt with the question of a peacetime economy." In contradictory fashion, war has spurred the creation and expansion of welfare programs, going all the way back to the country's first, short-lived federal welfare policy, which consisted of pensions for Civil War veterans and their widows. The welfare state of mid-century America was simultaneously a warfare state, its expansion accelerated by World War II. Today we still live in a proverbial guns-and-butter economy, where public investments in violence are enmeshed with public investments in care. After her husband was assassinated, Scott King dedicated herself to the cause of a federal jobs guarantee. Today the military is a far more extensive public job program than the Climate Corps, employing 2.1 million servicemembers and over 700,000 civilians. As Scott King argued, we need an economy based on meeting human needs and sustaining life, not manufacturing weaponry and promoting death.

Because racism has been key to undermining even the modest gains of the welfare state, antiracism must be a core pillar of the solidarity state. Today's war on wokeism is just the most recent version of an effort to break solidarity, roll back progress, and distract from our increasingly oligarchic economy. The right's plan for 2025, outlined in the Heritage Foundation's *Mandate for Leadership*, begins with fear-mongering about the "Great Awokening" and sets out to erase public discussion of racial justice, gender justice, the history of slavery, and the science of reproductive health. Given the centrality of the right's weaponization of racism—as well as misogyny, homophobia, and other forms of divide-and-conquer serving bigotry—the defense of racial justice must be central for a project that seeks a more universally beneficial alternative.

THESE PROPOSALS for the solidarity state are not a fully fleshed-out plan but a provocation and prompt, in hopes that intellectuals and organizers might find the seeds of something to build upon. The crises

Hunt-Hendrix & Taylor

around us are too severe to waste time, either on solutions too small or dreams too unreal. A solidarity state offers a potential horizon that is both feasible and transformative—and also more resilient against elite capture and reactionary attacks than our current paradigm.

Of course, states can both secure our freedom and threaten it; there is no way to permanently escape this dilemma. But the conscious cultivation of solidarity would make people feel more connected to each other and more invested in and protective of the social programs and democratic structures on which everyone's lives depend. Nurturing these relationships is essential to ensuring that vital progress is not lost and that our social debts—to past and future generations—are finally paid. Solidarity is both means and end, how we get out of this mess and where we might, one day, arrive.

Still from *The Long Summer of Theory* (2017). Image: Filmgalerie 451

THE SUMMERS OF THEORY
Peter E. Gordon

NOT LONG AGO and in certain small circles of academic life, the word "theory" conveyed a special magic. It signified both sophistication and freedom, elevating its devotees into a rarefied world of European ideas that would bestow the gift of insight into the hidden truth of language, or culture, or history.

Two meanings were intertwined even if they often ran at cross purposes. On the one hand, "theory" carried a hint of privilege, the cultivation of exquisite skills in reading and interpretation that were accessible only to an elite. On the other hand, it implied the hopeful idea of an emancipatory practice, since presumably anyone who wished to "do theory" did so because it promised, someday and somehow, to link up with the moral and political business of transforming the world. If theory was the question, practice was the answer. But even in the years of high enthusiasm for theory, the answer seemed forever deferred for another day.

Today, now that the passion for theory has been largely spent, it can be hard to explain why it was once felt to be so fascinating. Surely its exotic pedigree played a role. Theory, after all, was not the name for a specific doctrine; it was a serviceable if somewhat baggy term for various ideas and intellectual movements that arrived as imports from the European Continent. The high avatars of theory—Michel Foucault, Jacques Derrida, Jacques Lacan, Louis Althusser—were mostly French, and they had received a rigorous training in the European philosophical canon.

But when their work was translated into English, it seldom received a warm welcome among members of the Anglophone philosophical profession, who tended to see it as an interloper, an unruly child who had scant respect for the established standards of clarity or rational argument. It found a far more hospitable welcome in departments of literature, where it metamorphosed into "French theory," a rich brew of ideas that left many graduate students intoxicated if often bewildered, though it was best to keep one's confusion to oneself. In the 1970s and '80s theory swept through the humanities like a new gospel. Many were converted, some resisted, but few could doubt that they were living through a time of intellectual revolution. Like many revolutions, however, what began in hope eventually petrified into dogma. "Theory" became a fashion, and then lost its shine.

The Summer of Theory is almost the title of both a film and a book (in the film, the summer becomes "long"). They address a story that is far less familiar to Anglophone readers: how theory came to Germany, where it ignited passionate debate among intellectuals and artists and inspired new ways of thinking about literature and society. Both the film and the book are ingeniously crafted, and they are such a delight to watch or to read that they awaken summertime joy even as they speak to weighty themes.

THE FILM, by German director Irene von Alberti, is a brilliantly realized group portrait of three young women—Nola, Katja, and Martina—who share a flat in an industrial wasteland of present-day Berlin. The milieu is a little island of bohemia slated for destruction in order to make room for "Europacity," a slick new center for global capitalism. (In the years since the film was released, the development has come to fruition.) The protagonists are irreverent but earnest in their aims; they resist the allure of the new economy and thirst for creative expression, whether in the theater, in painting, or in film.

The film is by turns playful and bleak. The three women often encounter young men and pose the question: Is this particular man really necessary or could he just as well be a decorative floor lamp? They wave their hands and, zap: he's a floor lamp. In a more dispiriting scene, Martina presents her art portfolio to a talent agent who proceeds to mansplain to her about the meaning of her art while imagining how he can make it a commercial success. Confronted with the hailstorm of words she gathers up her art and quits the scene.

Von Alberti is an accomplished German director of strongly feminist convictions and a deadpan style of humor. *The Long Summer of Theory*, inflected with surrealism and touches of satire, harkens back to *La Chinoise, ou plutôt à la Chinoise*, Jean-Luc Godard's 1967 film that portrays young French Maoists who are plotting an assassination while recording their debates: it was subtitled *un film en train de se faire* ("a film in the making"). The result was a playful exercise in self-reference. In a well-known episode Godard films a conversation on a train between Véronique, one of the student militants, and Francis Jeanson, an actual professor at the University of Nanterre where the actress playing Véronique had been a student. Von Alberti, too, enjoys these tangles between fiction and reality. Nola is herself a young documentary filmmaker, and the film we are watching is the record of her efforts. She is shooting an earnest if somewhat rambling film on the topic of "self-optimized individuals and collective consciousness." The topic is meant ironically; what truly interests her is the question of whether there's any happiness beyond the immediate present. Lingering over the action is the echo of Lenin's famous question: "What is to be done?"

Unlike Lenin, Lola doesn't know what should be done. Over the course of the film, we follow her as she traverses Berlin, through parks and into offices and onto rooftops, where she conducts interviews with prominent German theorists (real ones, not actors) such as philosopher Rahel Jaeggi and cultural historian Philipp Felsch. Felsch is the author of *The Summer of Theory*, the book from which von Alberti has borrowed her film's title.

The connection between film and book is loose but instructive. Felsch tells the history of the German passion for French theory during the 1970s and '80s; von Alberti's film (and Nola's), is an open-ended inquiry into what guidance we can expect from theory today. While Nola waits for Felsch in a park to conduct an interview, she passes the time by reading his book. Over the course of their conversation, however, it dawns on her that the intellectual passions of the past generation may not be so easy to revive. "Have we now entered 'the long winter of theory'?" she asks. Have we given up on the old unity between reading theory and political revolt? Yes, responds Felsch. People no longer read with the intensity they once did. He describes a paradox: with the rise of social media, the entire public sphere is now awash in the written word. But to ponder all of that text would be a mathematical impossibility. Everyone writes, nobody reads.

Felsch is a brilliant stylist and his book is a true joy to read. Does this falsify his claim in the film? Nola is reading his book, after all, and she represents us. It is composed in a breezy and ironic style that takes intellectuals less seriously than intellectuals like to take themselves—describing not only their ideas but also their lifestyles and their affairs—but it is done with such deftness and wit that one seldom fears the ideas have suffered any distortion. To be sure, Felsch does not presume to be a grand theorist himself. Ideas for him are not candidates for evaluation; they are like characters in a play. His book is an exercise in intellectual history, not philosophy; he wishes to understand how theory became a fashion in Germany, how it arose and why it declined. But perhaps this is his point: if we are living in the winter of theory, the only task that remains for us today is retrospective.

To bring this tale into focus, Felsch organizes his history around the fortunes of a single publisher, Merve Verlag, an upstart little press founded in 1970 by Peter Gente and his wife Merve Lowien. The publisher's early books were all pocket-sized, often pirated or bootleg editions of brief texts translated into German from the French. Their titles could be enigmatic (like "Rhizome," a 1977 essay by French philosophers Gilles Deleuze and Félix Guattari) or deceptively simple (like the 1978 lecture-turned-essay "What Is Critique?" by Foucault). The first editions were cheaply made, stapled, not bound, and immediately recognizable by the minimalist but colorful rhombus design on their covers. The publisher still exists today, and in bookstores of a certain kind, one still comes across a full wall of Merve books in a vertiginous, multicolor display. But these days they are more often found in museum bookshops, and they no longer convey the promise of political utopia.

To focus all this attention on a single publisher may seem frivolous, but as a skilled cultural historian Felsch knows that what might appear marginal to an era can often define its center. The history of Merve Verlag is nothing less than the history in microcosm of a larger revolution in German intellectual life. (A similar story has been told about Semiotext(e), the pocket-sized press that specialized in translations of French theory into English, founded in 1974 by the late Sylvère Lotringer.)

BY THE MID-'60s, the ascendant generation of German students had already started to rebel against the official culture of political conformism and capitalist expansion that prevailed during the thirty-year period of economic growth known as the *Wirtschaftswunder*. Some looked for guidance to the Institute for Social Research (popularly called the

Gordon

Frankfurt School), an interdisciplinary group of émigré intellectuals such as Max Horkheimer and Theodor Adorno who had returned from America after the war. Admired by student radicals but vilified by conservatives, the Institute became an unlikely if inspirational force on the German left. Its theoretical orientation was vaguely Marxist but hardly revolutionary, since it saw the modern world as a fallen realm of near-total commodification in which there remained only the smallest glimpse of political possibility. During the war, Adorno had composed *Minima Moralia,* a book of lacerating aphorisms that braided together philosophical and cultural criticism in inimitable if often forbidding prose. Published in Germany in 1951 just after Adorno's return to Europe, the book became a kind of breviary for young readers and a model for what theory might be: essayistic, systemless, and ambulatory. Theory was a critical practice, or even a lifestyle.

The founders of Merve Verlag set out to create a publishing house that would follow this vision of what theory might be. But they also recognized that this would mean a rebellion in the ranks of the West German intelligentsia: they would need to free themselves from the authority of established German publishing houses such as Suhrkamp Verlag, the press founded in 1950 whose imposing books in philosophy and social theory stood as the very embodiment of the new Germany's left-liberal ethos. This was the spirit of enlightened rationalism and universalist ambition that readers would come to associate most of all with Jürgen Habermas, the philosopher who had once been Adorno's assistant in Frankfurt but who by the 1970s had emerged as the foremost representative in the second generation of Frankfurt School critical theory.

There was in fact an intimate bond between the Institute and Suhrkamp; the press would publish all the major titles by the Institute's members. The literary critic George Steiner went so far as to describe the left-liberal spirit of West Germany as "Suhrkamp Culture." In 1965 Adorno could plausibly declare that this was a "time of theory," and by the 1970s Suhrkamp had secured a wide readership for its academic series (the *suhrkamp taschenbuch wissenschaft*, or *stw*), which presented all of its paperback volumes in a sober and uniform dark blue. Among the first titles to be published in the *stw* series was the first volume in the now twenty-volume complete edition of Adorno's published works, released in 1970 a year after Adorno's death.

Over the next decade theory would change; it became more volatile, more experimental. When the editors at Merve Verlag began to carve out their own niche in the competitive world of German publishing, they found themselves pursuing a new and unfamiliar path that diverged sharply from the ethos of rationalism that made Suhrkamp such a formidable presence. One obvious change was a growing distance from Marxism. In its early years, Merve published its books in a series that carried the label "International Marxist Discussion." Later the series was rechristened "International Merve Discourse"—a sign of a certain shift in ideological orientation, away from the sober language of dialectics and toward the new theories that were imported from France.

The personal situation at the press also changed. When Gente met another woman, Heidi Paris, his first wife Lowien left the press (though it would retain her first name). Paris, younger and more venturesome in her interests, embodied the spirit of May 1968. Like many students of the time, she found Marxism sclerotic, a rigid system that inhibited the creative powers of the libido and the arts, and it was partly under her direction that the press began to read and publish works in translation by French authors such as Foucault and Jean-François Lyotard. Felsch assigns great importance to the activity of reading. Neither Gente nor Paris had the ambition to become theorists themselves; reading, they felt, was already a transformative practice. "Reading Foucault is a drug," Paris said, "a head rush. He writes like the devil." In 1976 she and Gente convened a reading group to make their way slowly through Deleuze and Guattari's *Anti-Oedipus* (1972), one of the more challenging texts in the new wave of French philosophy. The task took them five years.

What explains this enthusiasm? Part of the answer is surely the widespread perception on the left, in Germany as elsewhere, that the Marxist paradigm had been exhausted. The French translation of Aleksandr Solzhenitsyn's *The Gulag Archipelago* in 1974 brought to light the astonishing brutality of Soviet communism and helped to solidify new intellectual movements that were skeptical not just of capitalism but of all forms of rationalized institutional power. Foucault's *Discipline and Punish* (1975) typified this new vision of modern society as a total system of surveillance and imprisonment. The target was no longer a specific class or economic arrangement but the basic fact of social structure as such. Foucault saw that all attempts to introduce greater order into institutions only had the effect of enhancing their power, to the point where the human subject itself became complicit in its own confinement. In a conversation with French Maoists,

Foucault warned that even forms of popular justice were suspect. The simple placement of a table between judges and the accused was a sign of an emerging disciplinary society.

The waning of interest in Marxism as a social theory left in its wake an intellectual vacuum in which new passions could flourish. A major beneficiary of this change was the rediscovery of Friedrich Nietzsche, whom the Nazis had tried to fashion into an ideological forerunner, but who now appeared to German readers in a new and unfamiliar light. In a culture that was still reckoning with the memory of the Third Reich, the renewal of interest in Nietzsche's philosophy at home was possible only because it returned after undergoing dramatic reinterpretation abroad. French philosophers in the late sixties and seventies were reading Nietzsche with fresh eyes and without the burdens of history. In 1972 Lyotard gave a paper at a conference on "Nietzsche aujourd'hui" in Cerisy-la-Salle, in which he called Marxism "une dérive," a drifting off-course; instead he called for a principle of "intensity," a shattering of all hierarchies. He praised not politicians but "experimental painters, pop, hippies and yippies," whose lived experience "offers more intensity . . . than three hundred thousand words of a professional philosopher."

Gente and Paris were excited by this vision, and in 1978 they published a German translation of texts by Lyotard in a new hot-pink edition, *Intensitäten*, that became a Merve bestseller. Other lectures on Nietzsche followed, including a German version of Deleuze's introduction to Nietzsche. As Felsch explains, the overall effect of this new-Nietzsche wave was to introduce a spirit of playfulness into German philosophical discussion that Felsch describes as liberation.

"Those who read Nietzsche without laughing," Deleuze wrote, "have, in a sense, not read Nietzsche at all."

BUT IF NIETZSCHE brought laughter into German philosophy, the German Autumn of 1977 brought a wave of violence—kidnappings, murder, and hijacking by affiliates of the Red Army Faction—that threw the left into disarray. The Merve editors drove to Paris where they visited with Foucault and discussed the latest events. Their conversation, as related by Felsch, has been preserved on tape. Gente expressed his fear that, in reprisal for the terrorist acts, West Germany had turned into a police state; Foucault responded in terms that were somewhat baffling. Rather than addressing the particulars of the present crisis, he expatiated at length on broad points of history with allusions to the seventeenth century and the Sun King. The problem, Foucault said, was that the RAF still imagined that it was fighting an *ancien régime*. What it failed to recognize was that the nature of modern power no longer resided in the state. The urgent thing was to understand the "microphysics of power," the dynamic of a system without center by which power circulates throughout the social body.

After 1977, Felsch writes, "'theory' was not the same." Merve Verlag continued to publish works in translation, but its reputation for cutting-edge theory began to fade. Its gains in wealth meant that it could produce books in hardcover editions that were now shelved alongside other academic tomes in university libraries. With increasing frequency, Merve produced books of theory that exhibited a kind of aesthetic sheen that seemed best suited to the "white cubes" of the art world. For a publisher that had advertised itself as the outsider its success was not without irony. As Felsch says, "What it lost in its triumph was its aura of danger."

In the mid-eighties there came a new volley of criticism from Habermas, the doyen of critical theory, whose 1985 book, *The Philosophical Discourse of Modernity*, offered both a historical survey and a sober verdict on the failures of the intellectual avant garde since Nietzsche. The chapters on Derrida and Foucault were especially noteworthy for their vigor in dispatching these avatars of French poststructuralism as politically irresponsible and potentially irrationalist thinkers who were indifferent to the burdens of public-facing philosophy. Many found this verdict excessive and simply uncomprehending, but it laid out the terms of disagreement between critical theory and "French theory" that would endure for many years. Meanwhile, Merve Verlag underwent a shift in editorial leadership. Heidi Paris committed suicide in 2002; five years later, Peter Gente retired to northern Thailand, where he died right around the time that Felsch was finishing the research for his book.

Felsch has a knack for interweaving intellectual history with personal anecdote without descending into mere gossip. But for those who care most about the substance of the ideas, his narrative may occasionally raise the suspicion that the passion for theory in Germany was as much fashion as philosophy. Although Felsch does not dwell on matters of method, his book exemplifies a certain way of describing the history of philosophy without really doing philosophy.

To be sure, intellectuals, especially in the European or so-called "Continental" tradition, have long been aware of the fact that philosophy is not an exercise in world-transcendence; it is born out of history, and it is ultimately a practice of reflecting upon who and what we are in our own historical moment. As Hegel once said, philosophy is "its own time apprehended in thoughts." But there is a nonetheless a distinction between situating intellectuals in their historical milieu and entertaining the question of whether their ideas have any merit. With the skills of a cultural historian, Felsch has given us a vivid and often entertaining portrait of intellectuals for whom theory was not simply an academic exercise but a way of life. This is what philosophy has always been, from the Stoics to Foucault. But do we really need to know that Foucault was hanging out in Berlin nightclubs with David Bowie? Perhaps no, perhaps yes. One cannot help but feel a nagging suspicion that the passion for French theory became just a tad too self-conscious of its own status as a cultural trend.

It is this acute awareness of its own image that was responsible for turning the movement into what François Cusset called (in English) "French theory," a collective noun designating not a discrete body of ideas but a general sensibility that was brought to life only when it was packaged for export abroad. Cusset's book-length study of this remarkable phenomenon was first published in French nearly two decades ago, and it was clearly written for French readers. Its stated purpose is a sociology of the American reception, but its tone hovers between skepticism and (occasionally) disdain. For Cusset, "French theory" is a "weird textual American object," an interpretative monster that was the fruit of "decontextualization" or even "taxonomic violence."

He seems reluctant to accept that all intellectual activity involves a kind of translation, since there is no such thing as an isolable language or culture, and no theory or philosophical claim is so fixed to its native context that it cannot be moved and fire the imagination of readers elsewhere. As Edward Said once observed, "ideas and theories travel— from person to person, from situation to situation, from one period to another." What I mean and what you mean may converge but will never reach identity. The heroic work of the translator is not to reproduce an exact replica of the original but to broaden the bridges of mutual understanding. Shutting down those bridges would be tantamount to shutting down meaning altogether.

Felsch is more sympathetic to the many theorists and readers who populate his tale. Their aim, he explains, was "to cultivate Parisian philosophy in the German-speaking countries, not just in translation, but in native assimilation." Still, the attempt to turn oneself into a French theorist could easily result in "baroque stylistic lapses," a kind of playacting or mimicry where one adopted the mannerisms, both written and spoken, of *les philosophes français*. In the eighteenth century, long before anyone had ever heard of poststructuralism or semiotics, Jean-Jacques Rousseau had reacted with violent allergy to the affectation and theatricality of the Parisian salons. Those of us who lived through the twilight age of American enthusiasm for French theory in the late 1980s and '90s could often detect a hint of artifice when colleagues took up the new trend in philosophy with all the zealotry of converts. There were distinctive mannerisms, shibboleths or terms of art, by which the initiates could know their kin. In an era when irony and self-reference became commonplace tropes in literature and mass

Gordon

culture, it was hardly surprising that (to quote Felsch) "theory was becoming indistinguishable from the parody of theory."

For those who disliked French theory, parody became the preferred weapon. In a mocking 1986 essay entitled "Lacancan und Derridada," the professor of literature Klaus Laermann heaped scorn on the entire trend, accusing his German colleagues of "Frankolatrie." Among German readers the essay met with broad acclaim; it even won the Joseph Roth Prize for journalistic writing. Even better known was a 1996 incident in the United States, when Alan Sokal, an NYU professor of physics, resorted to a similar stratagem of parody, tricking the editors of the academic journal *Social Text* into publishing an essay that seemed to suggest that gravity was a social construct. Sokal knew that what he had written was nonsense, and some saw the episode as a scandal, the last nail in theory's coffin. But the amusement of such cases only goes so far; satire, after all, is not the same thing as rational argument. Theory may at times verge on self-parody, furnishing its critics a glimpse of an Achilles heel. But something is lost when one resorts to parody in lieu of critique.

PARODY MAY BE the final point of contact between Felsch's book and von Alberti's film. The slick art promoter in the film who meets with Martina—and who, when perusing her portfolio, nearly drowns her with jargon—is speaking in a language that sociologists Alix Rule and David Levine have identified as "International Art English," a specialist's patois that "drags around clichés of theory discourse wherever it goes." Felsch ends on an uncertain note, worrying that theory may be entering a winter phase. But he is too admiring to cheer its passing. He writes in a style of bemused neutrality, as if in the knowledge that all intellectual movements are destined to suffer the same fate: beginning with promises of radical transformation, only to shed their magic and cede their prestige when new trends come on the scene.

Perhaps Felsch's answer to Nola is right; perhaps we are living in a period of decline. There are good reasons to fear that the practice of reading difficult texts is disappearing. In the subways and city parks, more and more people are cocooning themselves in the private glow of their own digital cosmos. They do not so much read; they scroll. They also text and they tweet, but the Twitterverse is a place of combative self-display that bears little resemblance to Habermas's ideal of a public sphere.

All the same, the intellectuals who appear in von Alberti's film serve as good evidence that theory is not dead and that public-facing criticism continues to thrive. It is an unfortunate truth that the sort of theory that flourished in the last decades of the twentieth century eventually descended into scholasticism, where real questions of suffering and social transformation were obscured. But we should not mistake the fate of one intellectual fashion for the general fate of theory. Other summers will come.

CONTRIBUTORS

Gianpaolo Baiocchi is Professor of Sociology at NYU and Director of the Urban Democracy Lab. His most recent book is *We, the Sovereign.*

Jonathan S. Blake is Associate Director of Programs at the Berggruen Institute. He is coauthor, with Nils Gilman, of *Children of a Modest Star: Planetary Thinking for an Age of Crises.*

Joshua Craze is finishing a book for Fitzcarraldo Editions about war and bureaucracy in the Sudans. He is currently an Ideas Workshop Fellow at the Open Society Foundations.

Ishac Diwan is Research Director at the Finance for Development Lab at the Paris School of Economics.

Leila Farsakh is Professor of Political Science at University of Massachusetts Boston.

Janice Fine is Professor of Labor Studies and Employment Relations at Rutgers University, where she directs the Workplace Justice Lab.

Peter E. Gordon is Amabel B. James Professor of History and Faculty Affiliate in Philosophy and German Languages and Literatures at Harvard. His latest book is *A Precarious Happiness: Adorno and the Sources of Normativity.*

Joe Guinan is President at The Democracy Collaborative. He is coauthor, with Martin O'Neill, of *The Case for Community Wealth Building.*

Leah Hunt-Hendrix is cofounder of the Solidaire Network and Way to Win. She is coauthor, with Astra Taylor, of *Solidarity: The Past, Present, and Future of a World-Changing Idea.*

Mariame Kaba is an organizer and founder of Project NIA. She is coauthor, with Andrea Ritchie, of *No More Police: A Case for Abolition.*

Claudio Lomnitz is Campbell Family Professor of Anthropology at Columbia. His latest book is *Sovereignty and Extortion: A New State Form in Mexico.*

Martin O'Neill is Professor of Political Philosophy at the University of York. He is coauthor, with Joe Guinan, of *The Case for Community Wealth Building*.

Richard Pithouse is an academic and journalist living in Johannesburg. His work has also appeared in the *Mail & Guardian, CounterPunch*, and *Foreign Policy*.

Tara Raghuveer is the founding director of KC Tenants and the National Tenant Union Federation.

Thea Riofrancos is Associate Professor of Political Science at Providence College and a Strategic Co-Director of the Climate and Community Project. She is author of *Resource Radicals: From Petro-Nationalism to Post-Extractivism in Ecuador*.

Andrea Ritchie is a lawyer and organizer. She is coauthor, with Mariame Kaba, of *No More Police: A Case for Abolition*.

Hana Shepherd is Associate Professor of Sociology at Rutgers University, where she is an affiliated scholar at the Workplace Justice Lab.

Bright Simons is a social innovator and political commentator. He is Vice President of the IMANI Center for Policy and Education and the founder of mPedigree.

Olúfẹ́mi O. Táíwò is Associate Professor of Philosophy at Georgetown University. He is author of *Elite Capture* and *Reconsidering Reparations*.

Astra Taylor is a filmmaker, writer, and cofounder of the Debt Collective. Her latest book, coauthored with Leah Hunt-Hendrix, is *Solidarity: The Past, Present, and Future of a World-Changing Idea*.

Bonnie Tenneriello is Senior Staff Attorney and Solitary Confinement Project Director at Prisoners' Legal Services of Massachusetts.

S'bu Zikode is a founder of the Abahlali baseMjondolo movement.